Felony to
FREEDOM

Felony to FREEDOM

JOURNEY TO LIBERATING AN INSTITUTIONALIZED Mind

DESIREE "DEZI SPEAKS" RILEY

WALTON

Walton Publishing House
Houston, Texas
www.waltonpublishinghouse.com
Printed in the United States of America

Library of Congress Cataloging in-Publication Data under ISBNs herein:

Digital: 978-1-953993-23-6
Paperback: 978-1-953993-24-3
Hardback: 979-8-795726-22-9

Dedicated to the memories of Uncle Bill, Grandma Alice, Uncle Tony, Jazzy, Deon, Nana Grace, Sar, Aunt Chee Chee, and Aunt Carol. With the awareness that you continue to walk with us, we will keep working to make you proud. Thank you to everyone who has been running with us along this marathon journey. To the many loyal and supportive friends, family members, mentors, and colleagues, this could not have been possible without you.

You know who you are, and we will see you soon.

Love, Always.

CONTENTS

INTRODUCTION

*T*hank you for choosing this publication. I've wanted to write a book for a long time, and it seems divinity has caught us at the perfect points. As you move forward, you will definitely read some things that connect you with this story, but I hope you also discover insights that allow you to think new thoughts. No matter who we are, all of us have experienced hard times or moments where we felt that our lives were out of our control. We don't have to be physically imprisoned to confront an incarcerated state of mind. Soon, you will be reading about many of those very personal moments for me and the methods by which I learned to transcend such conditions when they reoccurred. There are ways we can experience bliss independent of our spatial location, and the same goes for misery. Together, we will navigate paths to personal freedom and sovereignty, which only present themselves past the liberation from mental chains.

My name is Desiree, The Well-Being Specialist, but most people call me Dezi. Currently "roadschooling" in Mexico with my growing family of nomadic overlanders. Overlanding means we prefer to travel over the road than via water or aircraft, and to roadschool means, the real world and its diversity is our most complete teacher. I am also a serial-CEO, creator, partner, daughter, friend, and mother of three beautiful humans, with another on the way. In 2012, I established my favorite and most impactful project, Young, Black, & Hustling LLC International Creators Community and Online Social Network. I have founded other entities worth mentioning, and further information about them can be found in this text. Throughout this book, I will share my journey from childhood to felony and then to freedom with you. Hopefully, by the end of this work, you will not only be familiar with my experience, but I also hope that you find intersections with your own life experiences and/or the opportunity to experience life through the mind of someone else. My journey is still one of much imperfection, but to me, the goal of life is not perfection but rather fulfillment.

I think that you're pretty awesome for experiencing this journey with me. I am looking forward to getting to know my readers over time, as you will now be getting to know me. If you stay to the end, I know you're a real one. Much Love. XoXo

Chapter I
FELONY.

Losing (Almost) Everything.

Off to Chicago!

y small gray Toyota Corolla was the least suspicious car ever. I was just able to purchase it brand new through a promotion offered to recent university graduates. Sporting black frame glasses and cute little pigtails, I could get anything done virtually unnoticed. After all of the recent hardships I had been facing with my son, this was just the kind of move that we needed.

"It's not hard to give up your power when you think you're powerless." (Dezi)

One evening in November of 2011, with my 5 year old son in the backseat, I pulled into the driveway of our Easthaven home rental and saw a young man rapidly tapping on the French entry door. We had been living there for about two years, and everything seemed peaceful until recently. As we approached the young man, he began asking if our dog had run away, so I thought he was being helpful as my pit bull had just escaped the night before. As we touched the door, the young man vanished. My son and I entered our home to find 2 or 3 other young men running from the living room and out of the rear sliding doors with our belongings. I was livid; our house was ransacked, and all of the recently purchased Christmas presents were gone. Memorable data storage, gone. TVs, appliances, undergarments, even a firearm – all stolen. Yes, our dog had also gotten away – again.

After we were burglarized, I decided that we should move to a safer neighborhood as our next-door neighbors were robbed in the same manner just three days later. Then after hearing more of the same reports from other neighbors, I felt so upset and violated that I ended up carrying a 40 caliber Smith & Wesson (that I randomly decided to hide the morning of the robbery) with me everywhere I went, by car. Naturally, with the relocation came an increase in living expenses, but I believed my son deserved security and peace of mind.

During this time, I was a student at Ohio State's John Glenn School for Public Policy and Management, working on a Master's in Public Administration. This program required that I complete relevant internships, including positions at the Ohio House of Representatives and similar entities. I was also responsible for maintaining full-time employment to keep up a household.

Over the course of that year, I had been building an independent financial services business. I knew this could be a path to increased stability and more time to spend with my son, who I wanted to homeschool. Following this plan, I was recently licensed to sell life insurance in three states and was working on acquiring a Series Six Investors license. The goal was to travel more and begin preparing other families for an optimal financial future as well.

Quality of life did begin to improve, but the financial burdens eventually became too much, and I was becoming desperate. There had to be a way to make more money. I had applied to every job I could think of, sometimes fifty per day - Nonprofits, Civil Service, US Military - anything that could bring more money to our family. I thought if I worked diligently at the part-time, temporary contracts I could secure, then I would surely be hired full-time. It turns out that sometimes you work harder and your job just ends faster.

I remember trying to join the US Marines for a good amount of time in 2010-2011. After months of engagement and testing, I was told that the tattoo on the back of my neck showed directly above our athletic uniforms' collar, which made me ineligible for the Officer Candidate School. So I told them I would burn the tattoo off and just enlist. Ultimately, that path did not work out, but I was determined to do everything within my power not to spend the remainder of my youthful years sitting down.

After our move in December 2011, I remembered telling a homegirl on the phone, "things can only go up from here!" Little did I know how wrong I was. My confidence in realizing the ideal future was fading more quickly than ever. With a very limited support system, something had to give. I was literally doing everything I thought I was supposed to do: getting the degrees, completing the training courses, racking up the internships, collecting the referrals, and building my resume while also trying to be a good mom. Still, there seemed to be no options available that would lead to any semblance of financial freedom. I decided to think outside of the box. How could I make money outside of this system without harming anyone?

The weekend before Valentine's Day 2012, I took my son to visit his father and family in Detroit, MI. This was a tumultuous and emotional visit for a variety of reasons. I remember it clearly as it was also the week that Whitney Houston died. While driving to Detroit, I was made aware of an opportunity to earn extra money in Chicago, and I decided that I needed to make that happen. We were already out of town, so I had no access to our usual child care support system. After requesting a few times to leave my young son John with his father in Detroit, that option was not made available, and I agreed to send his dad money when I received it, making it possible for them to reconnect soon in Columbus. They did not get to see each other very often, so I tried to do whatever I could to make sure they saw each other as much as possible.

It was late at night when we arrived outside of Chicago, and we checked into a no-frills hotel room. My son and I were enjoying this quality time together, and we watched old action movies during the brief stay. I prayed that everything would go well. The goal was to make it safely home and begin working to rebuild the many pieces of our life that had recently started to disintegrate following the robbery at our home during Thanksgiving week.

I awoke the next morning, eager to be finished with this mysterious mission to earn significant pocket change only by driving, and things definitely felt off. I decided to take John shopping in Marshall's, where I was instructed to leave my keys in the car parked discreetly in the lot. We returned to the Corolla about 45 minutes later with a bag of small boys' clothes and close to $42 in change. I pulled away from the parking lot, driving carefully because I knew I was likely involved in something very shady. Honestly, I was just looking forward to some sushi as it was my first day off of a two-week sugar shock diet that my new personal trainer suggested. Well, as you can imagine, I did not get any sushi.

When I first realized that the police were pulling us over, I quickly took care of a little business in the front seat and then turned right into a driveway that seemed to belong to some type of nature reserve or cemetery. The unmarked vehicle came right up behind me and directed me to turn my vehicle around. I knew they would search me because they had no reason to pull me over as I was intentionally driving perfectly. In that type of situation, you can't afford to do anything that might call attention to yourself. When they got to the trunk, I was hoping and praying that whoever just used my car had tried their best to conceal whatever it was that they did.

At this point, I was more than a little grateful for the still small voice that told me to leave my remaining firearm home before the trip to Detroit. Lo and behold, when the trunk was lifted, all I could see was a massive amount of marijuana, and the smell was incredibly strong. It turned out to be one hundred pounds of cannabis that were discovered in my trunk. Fortunately,

I was equally as surprised as the officers, which was a plus on my behalf. I was genuinely shocked to see that much weed, and I knew I was now responsible for the consequences. Immediately, I was absolutely sure that this situation would not blow over quickly. My careful driving did not save me, and having a child with me would not help the situation. Accountability for my actions was the only option. I felt sick but said nothing, even as they told me I wouldn't see my son again until he was my age. I was not Mirandized, and at this point, I wasn't quite sure how my words could be used against me.

I allowed them to escort us into a large black SUV that had just pulled up on the scene – it was outfitted with various technology. My son and I were driven to a local jailhouse on the outskirts of Chicago. Some members of the DEA interrogated me, and I gave them all the same clueless answers – "I don't know," "Craigslist, " etc. They were not tough with me beyond the initial confrontation.

The Illinois officers allowed us to wait for John's father to arrive, and he picked him up around 10 pm, for which I'm still very grateful. After my son was gone, I was finally escorted to my cell. That night was pretty chilly, and they had taken my jacket and other belongings: nipple rings, anti-EMF protection pendant, all my jewelry, my shoes, and laptop. I sat in the holding cell where there was a blank metal plank of a bed (if you can truly call it a bed) and a little metal toilet that didn't look like it was usable. Needless to say, it was a long night, but at least I was alone.

I wouldn't immediately call my mom because I didn't want to cause her too much stress. I was actually hoping to be out of this situation, back in my car, and heading back to my house before anyone else knew anything was happening. It wasn't until the next morning that I realized that I was facing up to 30 years in prison. I finally spoke with my mother and found out that she was told that I had shot a cop and some other nonsense. I suppose it was the kind of nonsense that happens when you don't speak for yourself.

My mom was relieved to discover that I was not a murderer but devastated that I was incarcerated. Soon enough, I was taken into the city of Chicago for the arraignment hearing. The public defender assigned to my case seemed to think that I could get off more easily since it was my first time, and I guess women in my shoes usually do things like this on behalf of their boyfriends, so they may get a slap on the wrist depending on the situation. When I walked into the courtroom, I spotted the two other gentlemen that rode with me in the police car to the courthouse that morning. I discovered that they were also involved in this same investigation and were possibly the ones who accessed my vehicle, but I was never certain. We ended up going to court together every time until my final date. On this day of the arraignment hearing, bail was set at $150,000, and I was required to pay 10% in order to be bonded out. I didn't have $15,000 and knew no one who could lend me $15,000, so I was definitely headed to Cook County Jail.

Everything that we did during each process took a long time – a long time in tiny, filthy holding cells. The prisoners were moved from one room to another at the courthouse like pack animals waiting to see a judge. When it was my turn to go before the judge, the proceedings went by so quickly that I could barely recognize if any of my loved ones were in the room. It went this way each time, and it literally felt like cattle herding. Then, we were finally herded downstairs to the buses that were to take us to jail, and we'd be given a nasty little snack with a juice bottle. The juice bottle is important because they don't give you a bottle to drink from when you get to Cook County Correctional Facility. Seasoned inmates know that when you're in court and you are given a juice bottle, you need to hold on to that bottle and not discard it. Unfortunately, I was not privy to this information and I did not keep my bottle, but we'll come back to this shortly.

When we finally got to the county jail, the bus pulled up in front of a descending ramp leading to a massive building on a giant campus. We exited the bus and were led into an entrance area for processing. They did the initial scan of our bodies to make sure that we didn't have any weapons or things on us that were missed by the hand searches of other officers, and then our mugshots were taken. After processing, we walked down long isles of bullpens where they were holding so many men that it resembled a slave ship. Finally, we reached the bullpens for females, these spaces were fewer in number and a bit less crowded. We then waited for another few hours, and by this time, all I wanted to do was see what my cell looked like, go to sleep, or just lay down. During our next leg of the intake journey, we arrived at a high school sized gymnasium and were given our so-called basic necessities, including shoes that did not fit most of their recipients. I also received a leftover size F bra and a pair of scrubs or jail uniforms. Apparently, the day I arrived, commissary orders had just been collected, so I couldn't place mine until the next week, which meant that whatever I ordered wouldn't arrive until the week after that. I ended up using the bra as a makeshift purse when I could get away with it. Literally, everything that the jail did not sell or issue was considered contraband.

So, those first two weeks were very hard without anything that was on the commissary list. Every day at lunch, you would receive a fake Kool-Aid packet as a beverage, and you had to mix it with tap water. If you didn't have a cup or bottle from the courthouse, you had to go to the bathroom and drink water out of your hands. This was really terrible because who knows how they treat institutional tap water in a city like Chicago?

Now and then, a kind person who recognized my situation would donate a condiment, let me borrow their tumbler cup or even a bar of soap. I was extremely grateful for this generosity. During the first two weeks, I ended up saving a single mayo packet to use as chapstick. I do not remember where I got this mayo packet, but I kept it safely folded in the pocket of my uniform scrub top. Clearly, my lips were too dependent on false moisturization. At this point, I really could not deal with the shock of going any amount of time without my lip gloss, and mayo was the best solution. On my first commissary order, I made sure to order my own tumbler, two chapsticks, more mayo, a fitted bra, underwear, writing supplies, and whatever else I needed and could afford.

I am forever grateful to my mother, maternal grandmother Jeanette Lewis, and uncle Michael Lewis, who made it possible to hire a legal team. They quickly gathered funds which were added to my limited savings so that I would not have to rely on the terrible public defender system. I was locked up with too many young ladies who had public defenders that did not know their names and didn't show up for court. These PDs are overburdened with cases while, many times, inmates stay in jail for months without actually seeing a judge. Some of these inmates are not even guilty of anything except being too poor to afford a bond or an attorney. Hence, they are guilty until they can pay up or wait to be proven innocent. I am speaking about the County Jail where you wait to be judged, as opposed to the prison where you're sent after conviction. Some people have been known to stay up to 12 years in the cage-like County Jail without much outdoor access or many other recreational and educational resources. For this inconvenience, inmates are usually granted time served doubled toward their final sentence. The dependence on the public defender system is what keeps so many people trapped in these institutions, cyclically – financial-based crimes with financial requirements for freedom. Most of these incarcerated people are also mothers and fathers. As it turned out, my attorney also happened to be friends with the District Attorney. Money talks.

It didn't take me very long to meet a few friends. We were all locked up and stripped of our belongings, so it was natural to find common ground. Of course, ego issues and fights arise in any situation where there exist extreme power struggles. But, when you're collectively brought down to your knees and there are authority figures talking to you like you're all animals, it's hard not to see one another eye to eye. Some guards seemed to come to work just to treat the inmates like trash. They used obscenities, disrespected our bodies, did all kinds of wickedness, and it appeared as if they forgot that they

FELONY.

were employed to serve. I will definitely say that some of the Correctional Officers were more institutionalized than the inmates.

Given that we weren't in prison, most people's stay at the institution was transitory – some for a night or weekend, others spent weeks, months, or even a few years, while most of the guards worked there for many years. I actually found myself in confrontations with multiple guards on many occasions, pleading for humanity on behalf of the women that were incarcerated. It got to the point that when disputes were handed out on our tier, I was chosen as the representative and given a stack of blank dispute forms. We had many issues, and I attempted to organize the people on our tier according to the respective problems. Some of the issues included a lack of jackets, available medicine, inmate medical neglect, the quarantine of our tier, and the inefficient temperature control that alternated between unsanitarily hot or freezing cold. I would write out a draft of grievances, and the other ladies would state their names at the top and the bottom of their forms and give the same grievances. Then in solidarity, we would turn in our grievance forms, which stated the same things.

I learned this strategy from working in politics and reading constituent letters as a legislative aide. I recognized the power of sending and receiving letters from a community or organization that all had the exact requests using the same words. As those letters rolled in, the message became really clear that someone wanted something done, and they had the strength of numbers.

Things went on this way for a period of approximately two months. One blessing is that I was also able to help a lot of my fellow inmates with pleading their cases to their judges. Many times, people are advised to write a letter to their judge, explaining what happened and why they may deserve another chance at freedom. The belief is that the judge will take closer consideration at your sentencing when you've explained yourself. I'm still not certain if this works.

19

Many people I met in jail hadn't met anyone who went to college or even had people to help them out with any kind of applications or letters. They were really grateful to have someone to sit down with them, listen to what happened, articulate how they wanted to communicate what happened, and put it together in an effective way that could potentially have a positive impact on their case. By the time I left, I had built many bonds, and there was like a celebration when I was released. Some people were crying, and we were all hugging and saying goodbye to each other until the door shut behind me; the first few weeks after my release, I actually missed them a lot, which seemed weird.

A lot of things were changing. While I was there, I was changing and not all for the better. Even when fasting and thinking about things that led me to conclude that learning lessons were necessary to get through this situation, I could feel myself adapting to a more street-based mentality. I made decisions that could have kept me there longer, and I realized that not only was I influencing my environment, but I was also significantly allowing my environment to influence me.

The day before I was released was the last day of a three-day fast. At the start of this fast, two friends and I had agreed not only to abstain from food but also from using obscenities and cuss words. On this day, we were on the tier watching Celebration of Gospel, and while we were watching the show, some ladies were talking on a balcony directly above where we sat to watch the television. We had a hard time hearing where we were seated, and they were speaking pretty loudly. Eventually, I got up, and I started cussing at these ladies and telling them to get away from the television if they wanted to have a conversation.

In jail, this type of communication is entirely normal, especially when you've been on the tier for a while. It's noteworthy to point out that most people that are sent to the county jail are in and out within a few days. They're not usually there for things that are considered serious. They're considered "fresh" and usually meet very few people. Many times they're able to pay their bond and are released pretty quickly. But the ones that are there for a while end up developing a tighter bond, with varying degrees of seniority. As a result, cliques started to develop, and because of the environment, the energy surrounding the cliques had a gang-like aura. I was even acquainted with a Ph.D. wielding incarcerated professional that went off on a disrespectful guard or two. The need to survive in an unfamiliar and difficult environment can cause anyone to behave in an unlikely manner.

"Don't you see we're trying to watch the f*cking Celebration of Gospel?" This was me cussing at grown women over a television program. It wasn't until I got out of that place that I wondered how I allowed that to happen. These women were people's moms, aunties, or sisters. These were adult women that I was yelling at and telling to go somewhere else because I was trying to watch a religious entertainment show. The ridiculousness of this hit me only after I left that environment. It still sounds crazy. But again, this was only one example of the crazy things that happened while I was there. There were more, and there were worse.

That situation taught me and continues to teach me to be true to your standards – who you say you are and who you want to be, no matter what environment you find yourself in. You can easily adapt to a more beneficial environment, but you can also adjust to a destructive environment. Adaptability doesn't only work in one direction.

On the last day of the fast, the same day as the television incident, I found out that I could be released by accepting a plea deal. The mere idea of freedom snapped me back to reality, as I was already making plans for my next three years in prison. I knew what classes I wanted to take and the purchases I needed to make for time to pass more quickly.

The following day I accepted the plea deal. During the exit processing, I met a young woman who was once a basketball player. She had to be approximately 18 yrs old but was clearly addicted to some hardcore drugs, and she was also heavily pregnant. Even though she was talking nonsense, it was evident that she was intelligent, but she had been through some awful things. She was tiny, and her stomach looked like a basketball on a broomstick, yet her spirit seemed very strong. Her whole highly extroverted demeanor just exuded pain – pain, and potential at the same time. We talked with each other for a few hours, and she was the last person I remembered meeting before I was released.

I left the building wearing my newly done natural hair micro braids and a random Akademics jacket because they couldn't find the jacket I wore when I arrived at the jail. I was blessed to have my good friend Carmen, who was like a sister to me, drive eight hours from Columbus, Ohio, to pick me up. She ended up waiting outside for over another eight hours because processing took so long, as usual. She picked me up and took me to an Extended Stay Hotel, shopped for a few groceries, and made sure I had some cash; she also gave me her North Face jacket. I stayed at the hotel for about a week; although lonely, it was very comfortable. In jail, I used to dream that I'd be waking up in my own bed, and when I got out of the county, I found myself dreaming that I'd be waking back up in jail.

At the time, the experience of incarceration was so impactful that it had seemed to overshadow everything I'd ever done or accomplished. I just knew that I would never get over it. After leaving the Extended Stay, I found a cheaper hostel – a cute, functional, and modern space. It was my first time staying at a hostel, and it was a very stark contrast to the county. There were very few white women in the county jail; I was surrounded by mostly Black and Spanish-speaking women (or Latinx, as people say these days). I even had to ask them, "Are there any white people in Chicago? And, how come they're not in here?" I may have seen one or two poorer ones who came in and stayed for a while, but, for the most part, the few who came in were out of there in a matter of one or two days.

FELONY.

I was the only woman of color at the hostel. Sometimes, a Black man would stop in, but there were no Black women. I was there for a while as I had to wait in Chicago for the judge to transfer my probation to Pennsylvania. In order for me to go anywhere else but Pennsylvania, I had to remain in jail and return for another court date over a month away. I was only given the option of transferring to Pennsylvania because the judge informed my attorneys that he thought it was best that I be returned to my home state and would soon be going on a 28-day vacation. There was a commercial around this time that said, "A bird in the hand is worth two in the bush." So, I grabbed the bird in my hand. Philly, it would be! My lawyers had told me that I would only be charged for possession, but the plea deal also included charges for manufacturing and delivery, and still I accepted that bird in the hand willingly.

At the hostel, I met people from all over the world who were full-time travelers. Hostel life was very interesting. There were many group events and shared spaces; no one else seemed to be there for a similar purpose as me. However, I was just grateful to be learning a great deal from so many new people, yet again. I was inspired to see that there were many people of all ages traveling the world and staying in affordable accommodations, and the experience helped me to gain an understanding of what a digital nomad really was.

I would have loved the option to return to Columbus, resume my normal life with my many friends and complete the Master's Program. However, I found out that you do not qualify for federal financial aid with a drug-related felony. I recalled participating in a re-entry employment class, and the instructor told me that a gentleman who had just served eight years for murder had a higher chance of being accepted into the military than I did. Sexual assault, violent crimes, and financial fraud are clearly more acceptable in this system than drug possession. Will this war on poverty, I mean drugs, ever end?

When I was finally transferred back to Philadelphia, it was sobering to realize that I had no friends or network there. I hadn't lived there since 2001, after 9th grade, before I moved to Ohio. This environment was almost alien to me, especially the social functions. I became depressed for a short while; I recall laying on mom's couch, just using social media the entire day. Some of my supportive cousins would come and try to encourage me to leave the house and do things. Eventually, I started boxing and created a hair supply company – Oya Hair & Health – selling "Brazilian" or "Chinese" hair weaves, basically Indian hair. This was not at all fulfilling, but it generated income. I also lived out one of my passions by joining a singing group called 'Koalesce.' Things seemed to be going alright.

The day before my 27th birthday, my mom called my cousins and me down to the kitchen. She wanted everyone out of her house as it was becoming too much having young people that didn't seem to be doing enough for themselves around her place. So, the next week I ended up getting a position at the asset management firm downtown. Later I found out that I was the first person they had interviewed. I informed them that I was a felon immediately after they offered me the position. Around that time Philadelphia had instituted a law where employers can ask about convictions during an interview, but the question couldn't be included on the application form. It seemed that most jobs in the financial sector weren't expecting felonious applicants or accepting paper applications. The interview with the lady who was to become my supervisor lasted three to four hours. She was very encouraging, and she seemed to really like me. She tried to do everything she could to get me hired full-time despite the felony, but I was hired on a probationary status as an intern until I could prove that I was trustworthy.

I was hired full-time after completing the probationary period. It was the best paying job that I ever had, as an Operations Manager and Senior-level Executive Assistant. It was the quality of company many people can only hope to work under. Yet, I was fully aware that I could not spend the remainder of my youth sitting behind anyone's front desk.

The incident which resulted in my incarceration caused me to reflect on my life, where I had been, the people that shaped my views, and the system that attempted to define me. I am and always will be so much more than what the world can see. We all are. During this process, I feel like I've searched for every thought I have ever had and sifted through every piece of knowledge that I have gathered because I want to leave you with something valuable. I want you to walk away with at least one message or two that will make an impact on your life. No matter where you are on the planet, no matter where you come from, I hope that something you have read here will stick with you.

The more I mature, the more I realize that I do not desire to be politically correct. It is most important to me to be aligned spiritually, to be authentic, and to share my true ideals. There are so many books you can pick up from any bookstore filled with words designed for political correctness. Respectability politics has not been my focus for a long time. When I was in college, collecting degrees, trying to make myself more acceptable, I still was not getting most of the positions for which I was applying.

 Kwēn Kunta
@DeziSpeaksLife

If you don't get the problem with mass incarceration, and other social injustices, by now...you never will.

#ontothenext

Chapter II
BACKGROUND.

More of the Tea

I have always considered myself to be a nomad. If my memory serves me right, my first road trip and relocation was in 1988. I was two years old, and I traveled from Philadelphia, PA, to Columbus, Ohio with my father (Leon), uncle Bill and my paternal grandma Alice. She was one of the hundreds of people from across the country relocating for a position at the newly built defense supply center. Her sons sought to avoid the poverty and drug culture that was destroying many young men's lives in Philly. Sadly, addiction cannot be escaped that easily. For most of my life, I've been moving from state to state, attended over a dozen schools, and learned to love life on the move. It was my grandmother Alice that showed me how to appreciate life on the road. She took me on my first trip to Disneyland, Hollywood, Atlanta, and many other places across the United States. Frequent flights alone became a thing for a while, but I mostly preferred road trips. I was about 16 years old when I organized my first independent road trip from Columbus to Philadelphia to visit my mom and go shopping in New York City's Chinatown. Luckily, I was able to carry good friends along with me when I traveled. We would return to school with the latest trends, usually imitation designer clothing, and handbags.

Raised as the only child to a hardworking single mother (Diane), I learned from early how to independently take care of most of my problems. I have an outstanding mom who was a registered nurse for over 40 years. She began her work as a Candy Striper medical assistant at 14 years old. As a Psychiatric Nurse when I was growing up, she mostly worked evenings, nights, and every other weekend. This usually left me with a lot of alone time, and I learned to solve most of the problems that arose, whether it be with boys, issues with bullies, or even my physical development.

I never really saw the purpose of seeking support for those types of situations, especially when I could take care of them myself. As I grew up, I realized that most people don't have those same circumstances, so my mentality regarding many things could be considered rare. My mom and I moved very frequently. She always stayed for the most part in Philadelphia, but even within the city, we moved about once a year from an apartment to a house, then back to another apartment. Most of the time, we moved around in the same area of the city, never too far from our family or church. This only fed my desire to move around in life.

Actually, I wouldn't call it so much of a desire as it was a norm. Traveling and constantly moving were a regular part of my growing up. My summer trips to Columbus, Ohio, every year were always a highlight for me. I would get a chance to visit my grandma Alice, my dad, and uncle Bill, and I was able to spend time away from the East Coast. Even though my grandmother's sons' drug issues did persist in Ohio, they both seemed a bit happier than when they were in Philadelphia. It was nice spending time with my dad even though he was no longer with my mother. I hung out often in the rougher areas of Columbus, where my dad and his friends resided. I would also get to spend time in a nearby suburb where my grandma eventually settled and bought a home that she designed herself.

My dad had friends that lived in the Greenbrier Projects area, a 52-acre property on Columbus' east side that once featured 122 three-story buildings.₁ This was pretty fun for me as a child. There were always plenty of children there and a few weekly social activities. I remember coming home pretty late one night and thinking it was fine, but it might have been about nine in the evening, so it really wasn't okay. He came down the street looking for me, very worried and visibly upset. He could not locate his 7-year-old daughter (it was the age before cell phones), and I noticed that he was crying. In retrospect, I guess he thought that anything could have happened to me while I was out there, especially in a culture that was so heavily saturated with drug trafficking. I remember one particular visit from Philadelphia to Columbus where my dad was badly beaten up – all bruised and puffy. I didn't comprehend what had occurred at the time, but apparently, it was related to drugs.

I slowly began to process what was happening when he was away for months at a time. My mom and my grandma would tell me that he was working in Dayton or Cleveland, and because he's a master welder formerly contracted by the US government, that was easy to believe. But he was incarcerated in some of these instances. They protected me and didn't want me to think of my father as a criminal, so they hid the truth. Even if they were honest with me, I would have loved him just the same. My father is a great man with a large heart and is very intelligent. He is extremely adventurous, athletic, talented, and he could build virtually anything. To this day, he possesses these abilities and is highly active. He has always loved me, of that I am certain, but the society and the culture in which he was raised and his childhood traumas made it so that he couldn't have the desired impact on my life that a good father like him would have wanted. I've always felt bad for him because of that.

BACKGROUND.

My paternal grandmother, Alice, did a stand-up job stepping into that space and filling the gap where he would have been. She helped raise me as best as she could and taught me most of what I know today. As a career US government auditor, she taught me how to take care of business, have professional conversations, manage logistical operations, and even how to manage a householder. Managing finances was one thing I definitely slacked off on when I went away to college. I typically prefer to learn my lessons the hard way. It works for me, but I would not suggest it to everybody. Many would say that it doesn't work for me either; but, that's their opinion.

The ironic thing about writing a book is that it costs to tell your story. There are many things that are too complicated to share. For instance, other people's feelings may be hurt badly, or it could potentially damage your reputation. The latter isn't so much my concern, but in terms of the impact my words would have on the lives of others, that is something I take quite seriously.

Let's say I know a little girl who was sent to live with one of her relatives. This relative was sweet to her when she went to visit and nice to all the children who visited her home. One year, the little girl's mother decided that she should live with this woman because the woman was so good with kids, and she seemed to have a beautiful life that she shaped for herself and her family. The woman promised the little girl's mother that she could correct her behavioral problems, as she had experience working in a juvenile detention center. From the moment the girl arrived at the relative's home to live, she was treated differently. Her mother did not 'whoop her ass' at home, and she was now in a house where corporal punishment was a multi-day occurrence.

At times the situation became so stressful her soul would vacate her body. Sometimes, there were people and children at the door, watching and laughing. The girl never found it funny when someone else was being beaten, especially if the spankings were harsh. So much dysfunction happened in this home, from prescription drug abuse to the forced abandonment of babies – just an overall high level of misery. The girl stayed in this home for three years, which seemed like a lifetime then. Each year she hoped that she'd be able to go back home to her mother, and it did not happen until the third year. That situation could have been worse than going to jail, especially for a child. She also felt much worse for the children that had to stay in that environment.

Everything is relative. It is very difficult when you come from a place where you're encouraged to speak your mind, and people aren't beating you, then literally transplanted overnight into a space where you are beaten with a belt buckle or a high-heeled shoe because you forgot a Sweet & Low sugar substitute packet. That type of occurrence can have a very dramatic impact on your life because the norms are shifted. There was no gradual exposure to the situation. It is like being tossed into a furnace without ever encountering flames.

If names or more specific details were included with the story above, individuals' feelings and relationships could be impacted or damaged. I do apologize if the review of such memories triggers a negative response from anyone who may have been involved in such a situation. Sometimes we remove the scab in order to heal properly.

I realized from early on that freedom of movement would also require financial independence through entrepreneurship. You would not likely be able to travel on your own terms with the finances to cover your expenses (without depending on a location-based job or permission from an employer) unless you are an entrepreneur. I knew that traveling was very important to me as it was almost essential to my personal happiness – it became something that I needed in my life. I understood that I would do whatever it took to be able to live a travel lifestyle.

By the time my son, John, was 11 years old, he had traveled all over the US, visited six countries on three continents, and had lived in two. People's mentalities vary significantly depending on the types of places they are from, and their thinking shifts as they emerge from their environments and get the opportunity to explore the world outside of their original habitats. In Philadelphia, PA, one of the largest and most impoverished cities in the United States, I've noticed a "just gotta make it" mindset from the people I encounter there. Being raised under systems of scarcity has caused people to live in virtual cages, sometimes with barely enough resources to survive, let alone the peace of mind to focus on the important goals of personal development and self-actualization. When all we can look forward to is making it through the day, the program of lacking has effectively handicapped our evolution. The ghetto, all over the globe, is truly its own kind of prison.

In 2008, Ohio State's African and African American Studies Department facilitated my first trip overseas. Some of my family members queried why I wanted to go to Africa so badly. I guess this was a little bit before pro-Blackness was considered "cool." Honestly, I had just become aware of the near extinction of our cultural identity within those recent years and was newly embarked on my seeker's journey. So, I could understand their confusion but would no longer identify with it. My classmates and I had just completed a 5-credit course in preparation for our one-month study abroad journey. I decided to dedicate my research to Christianity and its effects on Ghana. The qualitative data gathered sent me on a spiritual journey from which I've yet to return.

Years later, for my partner Levi's 26th birthday, I decided to plan a trip to upstate New York. A few friends, a cousin, Levi, and I drove from Philly to Accord, NY on a late Friday evening. The roads were super winding and unbelievably dark, and some of us were scared. We pulled into the property as instructed on our AirBNB directions and saw no one. The place looked abandoned, so I decided to keep driving around. Eventually, I spotted the boat (on land) and travel trailer we had rented for our "glamping" stay. We looked around and finally saw this man at the end of the driveway standing in the line of our headlights. All of us, being big-city kids, were seriously creeped out. Soon, he announced himself as the owner of the property and proceeded to show us around.

That night was very strange; most of us were cold, and the trailer was a couple of generations old. We were able to scrape up a meal with very limited cooked accommodations. While I'm not entirely sure how everyone else was feeling, I was finding ways to enjoy it. I've loved camping since I was a small child when my parents were still a couple. My father was once a Boy Scout and Navy Sailor, so nature activities were our thing when we were together.

We all decided to look around the 27-acre property the next morning. I had no idea that this trip was about to change my life forever. We discovered a large cabin with a barn, multiple other cabins, horses, goats, gardens, and a yurt. I had never before seen "Glamping," or Glamourous Camping, but this first encounter set the bar rather high. After meeting the owner and his wife, lovely people, we learned more about their story and journey. We were also offered an upgrade into a proper cabin, and the rest of our stay was amazing. There were a few more visitors, a small party, pizza from the outdoor pizza oven, and a jacuzzi in the snow. It was such a momentous experience for a group of city kids. The next month, on Halloween night, we returned as a family trip and stayed in the yurt. The second visit was even more mind-blowing. There was no wifi or fiber optic cable, but a small box TV with a few VHS tapes. For the first time, I saw broccoli growing from the ground and was able to pick our food to create our meals. I had the freshest collard greens I'd ever tasted in my life. I had no idea that life could be this simple and fresh. We fed the goats and talked to the horses, and my life goals were permanently shifted.

Being the business person I was, I started crunching the numbers as to how I could possibly make that lifestyle a reality. I would need more income and, clearly, I was spending it on Airbnb. After doing a little research, I began renting the beds in the common area of my apartment that night. Bookings began to flow immediately, and I was introduced to travelers from all around the world. Some of us would hang out or prepare meals together, and we were all learning so much. We even offered space to Couch Surfers on days when we had no paid bookings. The share economy was becoming my favorite thing ever.

At this time, we also had a big black Jeep Wrangler. It seemed that other people loved that car more than we did, so we rented it out on RelayRides (which is now Turo). Shortly after that, I hired my mother and cousins to become dog sitting partners through DogVacay and Rover. Between two homes, two cars, and four dog sitters, the path to financial stability seemed clearer than ever.

We were finally working out a strategy that would eventually end the anxiety-filled mornings of dumping my son to school early, so I could rush downtown and avoid being two minutes late for work. I worked for a Black woman-owned asset management firm in a downtown Philadelphia skyscraper, with billions of dollars of assets under management. There were benefits, executive access, and bonuses. The kind of job my family was proud of me for, especially after foolishly becoming a felon. I was honored to work there and still am extremely grateful for the opportunity. It was also during my time employed in the financial sector that I became aware of the emergence of Bitcoin. While I kept a watchful eye on the movement, it took me about a year to invest. Eventually, I was able to secure my first Bitcoin for $447. If you are familiar with the history of cryptocurrencies, then you would know that $447 per BTC is ridiculously inexpensive.

Through the blessing of this employment experience, I became fully aware that a sedentary lifestyle was not one that I could lead. Although I loved the company I worked for, and my supervisors, I knew I needed a change. It seemed like the best job that I could have been blessed with, but my physical being was literally dying. As a vegetarian, I still gained 40 pounds, and each year that I worked there, I seemed to look three years older. I spent hardly any quality time with my only son, and management still required more time and energy from me. Even though I was able to significantly tighten my administrative, communication, and marketing skills through this position, it was clear I had to execute the exit strategy.

December 31, 2014, became my last day working within Corporate America. I have called it Black Liberation Day. From that time, I've been on the mission of total independence. We landed in Belize, Central America, eleven days later. It was during our first magical visit to Belize and the Quintana Roo state of Mexico that I decided to fully relocate by that September. To say that we were budget travelers would be an understatement. Levi and I backpacked those first few weeks. We decided to simply explore and only book the first night stay in advance. Thanks to my final corporate bonus, I was also able to catch a few flight glitches that year. My son John spent his 9th birthday with new friends in Johannesburg, South África, and we expanded our network in Dubai, UAE. We accomplished our lifestyle through Airbnb and CouchSurfing, and we always wanted to stay at least two weeks while living like locals. During this period, The 'Revolutionary Travel Family' was initiated, as we began documenting our adventures and misadventures via social media.

Just Do It!

The biggest barrier is just to start. We were in Belize a few years ago, having serious financial issues. We ended up living at one with nature and learning to consume minimally. While much of that was great, I could feel myself falling into another bout of depression. I decided to get up one morning and just run, and the next morning, I did the same. Soon I began taking aerobics classes three times per week. That year I hit all of my fitness and productivity goals, and the hardest part was just to start. Turn pain into power!

The lessons learned while living in Belize for over two years and now in Mexico have been enough to fill a book. I will say that being in a situation where you can depend on nothing but your ability to network, strategize, and hustle was a total adjustment as an American millennial. The growth that took place within our whole family over the past six years has been monumental. I gave birth to our baby girl, Freedom, in the mountains of Cristo Rey, Belize, and then I gave birth to a son, Love, back in the City of Brotherly Love. Traveling is an amazing teacher.

So far, Mexico has provided the perfect pace for us. One reason we chose to settle there specifically was its proximity to home and the language exposure. As a roadschooling family, full immersion access to Spanish was a definite plus for choosing a Latin American country as a cost free way to complement our curriculum. This small city of Playa del Carmen, located between Cancun and Tulum, has been growing rapidly and attracting tourists for decades. Yet, it was extremely tranquil when we arrived in 2020, during the pandemic. Since that period, there has seemed to be a mass exodus of people from the US and other European-dominated countries (not only young people or people of color) who are beginning to call this area Mecca or Atlanta, Mexico. The Black travelers of this area are definitely putting on for our culture and making it all look so fabulous. New businesses, packed-out events, and community gatherings all have the feel of home while leaving you immersed in the unique vibrations of fellow freedom seekers. If you ever get a chance to visit a culture-based community, any culture really, I would highly recommend making that happen.

Travel, whether international or regional, can truly catalyze an awakening experience. We should not underestimate the value of leaving one's original habitat and expanding our minds to recognize the differences between our lives and the lives of others. There is also a strong recognition of familiarity, especially when exploring among local populations. The impact of this experience would certainly vary depending on your origins and socioeconomic background, but either way, the discoveries made can be life-changing. While there is nothing wrong with resorts or tourist attractions, the same information can't be gleaned as with a more authentic travel experience. I think if you're confined to a compound that resembles Miami or LA in amenities, accommodations, and pricing, you may as well be in Miami or LA. This is one reason we typically prefer vacation rentals in family-friendly local neighborhoods wherever we travel. Even though a sweet all-inclusive is an appreciated luxury now and then!

The Airbnb branch of our shared economy business died after dozens of positive reviews over the years when Airbnb deactivated my account due to a seemingly random background check in 2018. This was a devastating blow, especially for a crime that people are legally profiting millions from now. We have since been in contact with the American Civil Liberties Union regarding this matter – and life goes on. My next goal is to purchase an RV or converted bus to tour the US and Central America with our intellectual property and merchandise – one step at a time.

Business Mindset

I've always had an entrepreneurial spirit. While a student at Independence High School in Columbus, Ohio, I would purchase bulk candy from BJs and Gordon Food Services and sell it from classroom to classroom in a giant colorful Limited Too tote bag. Looking back, I'm not even sure how the teachers allowed me to do this. However, I can recall that everyone was more than supportive, and my classmates truly enjoyed the candy delivery services, especially after lunch.

During my first year at Grambling State University, I was able to finance most of my activities by selling faux handbags and nameplate belts online and from the trunk of my car in Louisiana and Texas. At this point, I still hadn't quite taken myself seriously as an entrepreneur. I just knew that I was doing what I had to do to cover the expenses for the things that I wanted. I was the only person I knew who could live off-campus as a freshman and also have a vehicle that I used to travel in and out of town. Technically, I was able to live off-campus because I was legally classified as a ward of the state in 2001. This was not only enjoyed by me but my growing network of schoolmates and my new sisters at Sigma Alpha Iota International Music Fraternity for Women. Having a car and an apartment off-campus made our pledging process more interesting. I'm eternally grateful for those experiences.

When I transferred to The Ohio State University following Hurricane Katrina and the birth of my first son John, I began to shift my focus more toward community and public service. I walked away with two Bachelor's degrees, one for Humanities (African & African American Studies) and the other for Social and Behavioral Sciences (Political Science). Just before I was arrested, I was five classes away from completing my MPA at OSU, which I planned to combine into a dual degree with the Juris Doctorate and a focus on Administrative Law. That plan has not been completed.

Kwēn Kúnta
@DeziSpeaksLife

what happens when you realize your entire life is based on what other people told you to do?

Chapter III
CHOICES.

Tests of Character and Personal Development

*I*t was odd when I decided to write this book because I do not enjoy talking about my trials and accomplishments. I do like to talk, but I rather discuss things that are happening in society, nature, and sustainability for the future. However, when it comes to discussing the past, I become a lot more close-mouthed. I do not think I have always been this way. I believe the bulk of these feelings stem from the paranoia of being incarcerated and knowing that it happened because of an investigation by law enforcement that directly led to my arrest.

It means that I was under surveillance for a while, with my child, and that information had led me down a rabbit hole of paranoia. Knowing that I was watched to any extent and that the outcome could have potentially ruined my entire life makes me think more than twice about my choices. Now, I don't want to do anything that could get me into serious trouble, and I don't want to take the risk of losing my children for any amount of time again.

While Child Protective Services didn't take my son, one of the most precious things I lost during my incarceration was spending time with him. Sure, I lost my car, house, furniture, and everything that was stolen and seized by the government – but losing time with my son was the most heartbreaking thing that happened while I was incarcerated. It was the only thing that made me shed tears. While I was locked up, I missed my son's sixth birthday, and that hurt so much. Unfortunately, even to this day, I feel like I carry an unhealthy level of paranoia in many circumstances. I've tried to allow this to convert itself into pronoia by essentially creating positive karma for myself and doing things that I know could only benefit our lives in the future.

That mindset hasn't made me trust in other humans or anything else much more. Loyalty is something that's very important to me. I believed that loyalty was everything while I was locked up; it was my mantra – but loyalty is not everything. Love, life, creation, that's everything. Loyalty is a very big part, and any bond to me without loyalty is not a bond at all. I would say that maybe it is a bondage and definitely a burden.

I try to intentionally build an inner circle that values loyalty as much as I do because my aversion to betrayal is serious. I've made my circle almost non-existent at this point, just my immediate family, some cousins, and a few friends that I see every few months or so; I prefer things this way. Even though I value building community, it is very hard to let people get close when the majority only value what you can do for them.

It is such a blessing and so refreshing when you can connect with people who genuinely like who you are. They value your contributions to any situation, and those same feelings are reciprocated when it's not a parasitic but mutually beneficial relationship, one where they're not pretending to appreciate you for some future gain. I value those connections, but until they become more common, I'll enjoy having a very small circle.

I'm also learning that it's best to share too much than too little when writing a book. So, these are my most honest and genuine thoughts poured out to be published and shared with the world. This takes extreme vulnerability and trust, and it's also a healing journey for me. I know that paranoia is not healthy, and I know that isolation is not always beneficial. I want to grow and improve on my weaknesses, personal limitations, and flaws. I want my children to grow and feel free to share with, trust, and love other people, but I believe that healthy balance and awareness of the world are equally important.

I've always seemed to be closer to my elders than people my age. I think this was in part because I was raised by elders. For a while in 9th grade, I also spent time living with my maternal grandmother Jeanette. She is now approaching 99 years old and is the definition of a matriarch. We were all raised to revere our elders and placed them in an almost god-like status. She raised a family full of people that work hard and have a high level of integrity, for the most part. My uncles are some of the best men I've ever met, and I'm grateful for that. Grandma Jeanette is a very strong woman, born in a deep southern family, she lost her sisters and mother very early and was mistreated by her father physically. Even though she had to leave school prematurely to manage new responsibilities, she's an absolute genius. Through fundraising, she acquired over a million dollars to fund the purchase and maintenance of our family's home church. Our family has now founded a church called "Assembly of Love" in Philadelphia, PA. It's growing and constantly serving the community.

My life has taken many wild twists and turns. From the perspective I initially saw myself, I never imagined being in the fortunate situation I'm in now. While I was in middle school in Philly, I began shoplifting at hair supply and department stores. At that time, I did not believe I was happy with the person I could see myself becoming. I remembered a young male friend of mine eventually taking notice of the dark rings around my eyes. Even though I could feel their weight, I didn't know they were quite so visible. My mom used to say, "Dee, open your eyes more! You have such beautiful eyes." My face continued, unchanged; not really sure how to describe this period. Maybe I'll just call it urban adolescence.

During this season, I thought I was saving money or taking things I "could not afford" from people who had a bunch of money. Luckily this period in my life didn't take too long to pass. Soon I started losing things that I already cherished. For example, I would look for a blouse that I loved, and it would be missing. I chose to believe that this was because I had been stealing and making my mom's life much more difficult. Then I figured that if I simply stopped stealing, I could keep what I earned and really wanted. This way of thinking has continued to work out for me. I shared this because some of you may have experienced the same thing or have a young person in your life who is experiencing the same thing. This period just felt dark.

When I relocated to Columbus, Ohio, to live with my paternal grandmother Alice following my mother's brief mental health crisis in 2001, I began making new friends. Not only were most of these people more hospitable than I was accustomed to and a lot more community-oriented, but many also had a higher level of innocence than I had experienced in Philly. It seemed as if they were better preserved from the harsh realities of poorer urban environments. I ignorantly mistreated a couple of my high school boyfriends, who were very good people, due to my trauma-based belief that males don't really have feelings. Shortly after high school, I was tested with the most stressful relationship I could have thought possible. When I was about 21 to 22 years old (after a child, years of cohabitation, and a canceled engagement), I decided to wait for what was suitable for me while developing myself into a more suitable mate.

I have made many poor decisions based on my desire to speed to the "next level" in life. Everything felt like a competition because I had been counted out so many times since I was a young child due to unaddressed trauma and conflictions of self-worth. The rise of social media only exacerbated the issue – I had to win! Whether it was to win a terrible mate, win a job I would soon hate, or win a title I didn't really want to hold – I just had to win. I was very thankful to have learned in my most recent years that I am only competing with myself to become the best version of myself. I am honoring my path, the lessons, and the connections, and I feel extremely blessed that I no longer want things that are not for me.

We must remember that everyone we read about, see online, or watch on television is only human. These people have made choices or have been surrounded by others who made choices that led them to wherever you discovered them. The life that we desire, within reason, is a responsible set of choices away. No one is any better than we are; some are just more dedicated to their goals. There is no reason to want their lives or idolize them.

Healthy Minds. Healthy minds make healthy choices. Too often, we self-medicate from the pain we still feel and memories of neglect. We self-medicate using addictive substances or behaviors like food, drugs, sex, gambling, productivity, social media or being overly busy as a way to escape from our realities. These are coping mechanisms to deal with those feelings, the stress that comes after the trauma, and the trauma that comes as a result of the stress. While my childhood wasn't as bad as many that I know about, I noticed that many of the behaviors I display in relationships and parenting deal directly and correspond with interactions I've experienced in my early life.

Often, we disregard our issues because we believe they're not as deep as other people's or as bad. We tend to compare them and validate them against the level of tragedy other people have faced. When we do that, we don't give ourselves time to properly heal and adjust to the truth of what we have experienced and are still experiencing because our experiences are valid, and they do matter. They shape who we are and the person that we will become. They also shape the kind of people that we will raise and the people we are presently raising. So, in order to possibly self-heal, we have to acknowledge all of these things. It causes us to dig deep and lift scabs, uncover band-aids and wounds that haven't actually healed but may have just been concealed.

Throughout this work, you'll notice much repetition. I believe repetition and story-telling are necessary when trying to relay relatively abstract messages. The more the concepts are repeated, the easier they are to process the next time they are read. Messages in written words communicate directly to the subconscious mind as letters are the evolution of symbols. Symbols are solely created to communicate to an audience without them absorbing the message more literally, as such became the advent of written language.

When I am discussing healing, the frequency will be increased. Healing is so important because, without it, old wounds remain open. They will only fester over time when they are covered and neglected, much like a gunshot wound hidden behind a sleeve. The sooner painful and damaging issues are addressed, cleansed, treated, and healed, the better our lives will be. Making self-healing a habit can be one of the most beneficial skills any human can develop. We can take these practices and help heal others or even pay the information forward. We can share the steps that we've developed that helped us most effectively. When old injuries leave scars, that new skin is now much thicker and stronger.

This is important because this guide is not about me telling you all the answers as if I have it all figured out. I just turned 35 in June of this year, 2021, so I know I don't have all the answers. However, I want to share what I've gathered so far in this journey that I'm on right now. Maybe, I'll write a follow-up book, but at this point, I want to share what I have already found out. Perhaps, it'll be channeled through another art form next time, but hopefully, it will add value to someone's life. If it impacts just one person on this planet, I feel like it's done its job. Even if it only impacts somebody 300 years from now or 2,000 years from now, I've done my job. I feel like it was worth it.

I'm grateful for those who read it today and who will read it tomorrow, and I'm thankful for those who will share it. I'm grateful for those who embark on their journey of self-healing through reading these words or listening to this audiobook. I'm thankful for all of you for being alive, being resilient, and choosing to consume the content you think will benefit you. If you haven't heard it enough, I am proud of you. Too often, we don't hear those words of encouragement. It's important to let other people know that you're proud of them, especially when they're trying to do the right thing for themselves and their community.

I honor you; I respect you. I hope you can honor yourself, respect yourself, and do what you believe is right, even when it's inconvenient and when people disagree with you. The right thing is not always popular, and most times, it's not popular at all. I encourage you to continue to think critically and think for yourself. It's not something that's taught or even seemingly valued in this global society, but it's very important as we discuss the path to sovereignty and independence. I'm nowhere near as far on this journey as I hope to be, but every day, I feel closer. Hopefully, the progress is measurable month by month, year by year.

As I communicate with you at this moment, I feel progress. I'm grateful for you for getting me to share in ways I'm not typically comfortable and talking about things I usually avoid. I'm thankful for your time, energy, and your support. Many thanks, much love!

Choice
noun

1. **an act or instance of <u>choosing</u>; selection**:
   Her choice of a computer was made after months of research. His parents were not happy with his choice of friends.
2. **the right, power, or opportunity to <u>choose</u>; option**:
   The child had no choice about going to school.
3. **the person or thing <u>chosen</u> or eligible to be chosen**:
   This book is my choice. He is one of many choices for the award.

4. **an alternative**:
   There is another choice.
   adjective, **choic·er, choic·est.**
5. **worthy of being chosen; excellent; superior.**
6. **carefully selected**:
   choice words.[2]

"Between two evils, choose neither; between two goods, choose both." (Tryon Edwards)[3]

There's an Indigenous American tale that goes that within each of us are two wolves, one good and one evil. The way to determine which wolf grows stronger depends solely on which wolf you feed the most often.

Choosing which is the right decision is often relative to the decider. However, my concept of "right living" is the conscious choice to behave in a way that is most beneficial for society at large. You can choose not to litter or be a disrespectful person, and you can choose kindness toward animals and all things vulnerable, to honor our elders, and to protect the environment. The list goes on and on. All spiritual systems have some level of "karma" attached. The Law of Attraction magnetizes toward us the type of being we choose to be. If we choose misery, misery will prevail. If we choose generosity with the right intentions and wisdom, abundance is an eventual consequence. Every sentient being has been blessed with the ability to choose and to control our chosen thoughts. Decisions become habits and patterns which form our overall character; making the right decision becomes easier with time.

"Ideas matter. The world matters. Our lives matter, and the choices we make as we navigate our lives perhaps matter most of all." (Lauren Myracle)[4]

Most people want change, but few people want to change. Our choices impact lives, they change the world, and they shape ideas. It's a huge mistake to think that your choices don't matter. You are a result of your choices, and you are the only one who can make your choices. This must be 'innerstood' in order to achieve sovereignty.

It feels like I am giving birth to this publication. The idea of exposing more of my innermost thoughts makes me anxious sometimes. I can see myself continuing to grow daily; even on a momentary basis. At this time I am forced to do introspection that I never found a reason to do because I keep so much inside. I choose to share what I do because I feel like this is being crafted specifically for people who already have some familiarity with the situations I have grown through. If all of this is very new to you or you lack awareness about the realities that people from marginalized communities experience, then many of these messages may not be for you.

However, I appreciate you staying to read them because it shows that you are interested in expanding your consciousness by learning through the experiences of others. It is important that the populations directly affected by the issues that I discuss here have the opportunity to embrace the concepts outlined in this content. If you purchase this book or someone gave it to you, and you feel that someone else could benefit that may not have the resources to buy it, please, please, please share it, pay it forward, send it as a gift, and add it to your local library. Maybe it will matter to and help someone.

The purpose of writing and publishing this guide is for impact. I want this work to matter and last much longer than I will. I hope that someone in the future can better grasp and understand the realities of the 20th and 21st centuries by reading about these stories and digging into books from authors with similar experiences. When I was in jail, I was so happy to have books, and I read more than ever during that period. Two of my favorite books were one about Navajo Code Talkers and another about Geishas. Through those books, I learned so much about other cultures. Books became like Christmas gifts that allowed me to travel through time and space.

I discovered more about the forced assimilation of the Navajo Nation and how the same language that was attempted to be stripped from them was one of the only things that helped the United States during WW2 because their codes could not be deciphered by enemy spies. In the book "Woman of the Silk," I learned how young geishas would travel long distances to generate income for their families and about the issues they faced: danger, oppression, sexism, and poverty. Although I read these books many years ago, the impact that they continue to have on my mind and belief systems is significant.

It was so nice to understand people's lifestyles generations ago from various cultures, simply by reading words on paper. However, I know some people may hear of this type of content and immediately begin to make judgments. Their preconceived ideas and level of self-righteousness make it so that they have to be able to look down on someone else. These types of stories reinforce imaginations of their superiority, and if that is the reason you are reading, I really hope that you discontinue, period. I am not expending energy and effort in baring my soul and expressing myself as a sacrifice to build up your false identity and an oversized ego.

Now that we're clear and that message has been sent, I will focus on the people that matter. Let's dedicate our efforts to the people who do support us, that are looking for ways to benefit from our journeys and are looking to build upon the ideas expressed within the message and follow that flow.

I, for one, know that I've spent too much time in the past being disappointed when people did not support me or if people criticized my efforts without offering any actual solutions. Then I realized that, in those moments, I was not showing enough gratitude and attention to the people who have always shown me support, the ones that never left my side, and the people who always had my back. There came a time when I decided to dedicate my life to those people and dedicate my work to the people who will help fulfill the purpose in the end. Those are the ones I want to build with.

I don't care who is doing better than me. I am doing better than I was last year.

It's me vs me.

Chapter IV
PRINCIPLES.

Methods and Ideologies to Govern our Lives by for the Most Beneficial Long-Term Outcomes.

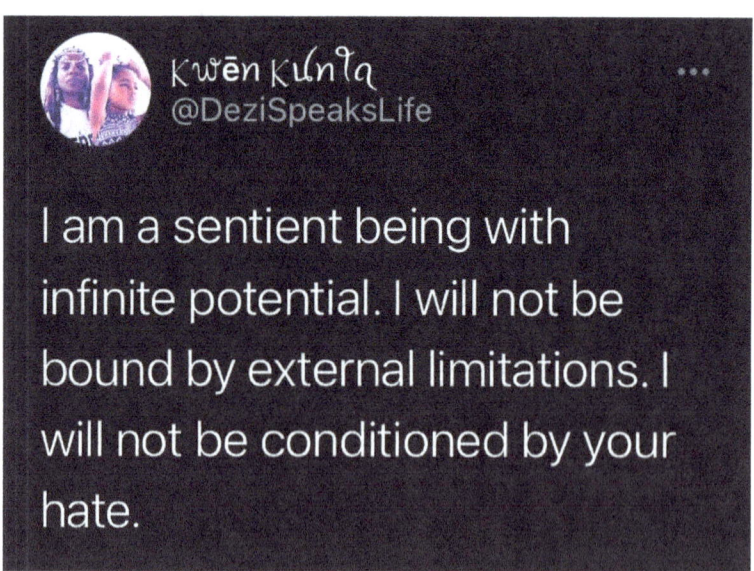

Kwēn Kúnla
@DeziSpeaksLife

I am a sentient being with infinite potential. I will not be bound by external limitations. I will not be conditioned by your hate.

I'm usually wary of any one-size-fits-all philosophy, but the concepts outlined below have proven themselves to be universally true throughout all known generations.

Principle 1: What You Focus on Grows

We become what we feed our attention. It's important to carefully and intentionally cultivate the types of content we want to consume. We possess ear gates and eye gates, along with mouth and nose gates. Since we have the power to control what we look at and listen to, we also have the power to decide what is allowed to take place in our lives. The things we choose to eat and smell can increase toxicity, or they can induce healing. It can't be overstated that we must be intentional about everything if we are seeking to achieve personal freedom. Personal freedom is not for the person who only wants to live a comfortable and convenient life. There is nothing wrong if that is what you want; just know this information might not be speaking to you. Through discomfort and developing resilience, we grow into the highest version of ourselves.

At our fingertips is the power to destroy our lives or create the lives of our dreams. Some people's choices on their cell phones cause them to destroy their families, lose their jobs, homes, reputations, and everything. Other persons might have the same cell phones, Wi-Fi, or cellular plan and instead choose to build a multimillion-dollar business. It's all about the content that we deliberately choose to consume or create.

> **"What you focus on grows, what you think about expands and what you dwell on determines your destiny."**[5] - quote taken from the blog "Hypnotherapist & Life Coach" by Monika B.Jensen PHD

I like to think of life as a buffet; there are so many options to consume. Think about the buffet tables that are packed with many people. What are they usually serving? Think of the buffet tables with the smallest crowds. What's being served on those? Is it usually best to consume what's most popular? What will actually serve you, your being, and your future the most healthily?

Principle 2: You Feed More Than a Body

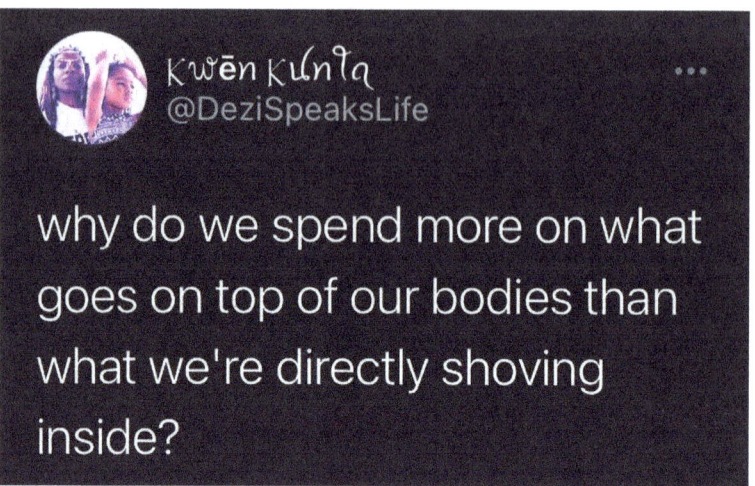

> "You can tell by a person's health how they feed their bodies. Those who are overweight usually over indulge; allow their diet to be fast foods. The majority of people are aware of the importance of proper diet. You know what you feed your body, but on what do you feed your mind? Feeding your brain is as important as feeding your body!"[6] - quote taken from the blog "What Do You Feed Your Mind" by Catherine Pulsifer

Guard the Gates. About a decade ago, I decided to "bombard myself with positive propaganda." This propaganda ranges from my obsession with vision boards (online & physical media), cut-out quotes taped to my walls & mirrors, posting pictures of beautiful scenery and healthy foods on my walls, desktop, and phone screens, and most importantly, blocking content online that I did not want to see while following things that were most beneficial. It can take days, months, weeks, or even years to notice the obvious changes, but just as with the online algorithms, the transformation begins as soon as you start.

We can control our thoughts. Practicing that control becomes easier with time. The mind is a muscle, and like the rest of the body, it can operate more fluidly and efficiently with proper exercise, rest, consumption, and nutrition. The soul, connected with God, will now possess a much more balanced vessel. Our soul will have a more proficient mechanism in which to help us navigate our daily lives.

Principle 3: Changed Thinking Changes Lives

"If you change your thinking then your life will improve. But, what thoughts do you change? Your bothersome thoughts about a position can simply be found in your self-talk. Self-talk is that inner running conversation you have with yourself. It is what you tell yourself about life's situations."[7] - quote taken from the blog "Hypnotherapist & Life Coach" by Monika B.Jensen PHD

Sometimes we feel like the world is against us, yet we're often our own worst enemies. Most times, other people are too consumed with the thoughts running wild in their own minds to constantly watch someone else. That's why focusing on developing more optimal internal processes and thoughts should be one of our highest pursuits.

It is entirely possible to take control of our thoughts. They are not as involuntary as breathing, which can also be controlled with practice. Actually, once we become aware that we can control our thoughts, it becomes irresponsible and neglectful not to put in the effort. Our thoughts are things that possess matter, and they are real. They make things happen, to our benefit or detriment, that affect not only us but those in our circle of influence, and so on.

Principle 4: Transformational Power in Collective Thought

> "For where two or three are gathered together in my name, there am I in the midst of them." (Matthew 18:20)[8]

There is surely strength in numbers. If a critical mass decided to think intentionally toward a collective focus, the world would be changed. The science of noetics (which covers the field of thinking and knowing, thought and knowledge, as well as mental operations, processes, states, and products through the data of the written word)[9] explains that as increased masses of consciousness tune into a certain potential (event or outcome), it allows that thoughtform to become an actualized reality.

"**Bridging Science and Spirituality.** Today, The Institute of Noetic Sciences trains the lens of science onto noetic phenomena such as these to gain a deeper understanding of the interconnected nature of reality. How can we better access this place of inner knowing? What are the practices that enhance our experiences of transformation, innovation, and well-being? What can science reveal to enhance those practices? How does this positively transform our lives and create a better world for all?"[10]

A generalization of one of their primary pillars outlines that as more people concentrate on anything, the easier it is to manifest. This science, or universal law, can be used to our benefit or to our detriment. It can be utilized by us or against us.

> "The day science begins to study non-physical phenomena, it will make more progress in one decade than in all the previous centuries of its existence." (Nikola Tesla) Inventor and Futurist[10]

"The evidence suggests that shifts in collective consciousness occur (such as when many people suddenly pay attention to the same thing) may influence other people's awareness, behavior, and perhaps even aspects of physical reality itself. This project builds collaboration between experts in the field to synergize our efforts in answering questions about collective consciousness effects on the physical world."[11] The world is already being changed; everything is always changing. The only thing permanent is change. God cultivates opportunity for constant change. We are not victims to change; we are created to help direct change.

Principle 5: Everything Will Always Change

Another thing I learned from moving around so much as a child was that nothing is permanent. All the friends that I made and almost all of my relationships were transitory. I could make a friend for one year and never see that person again for the rest of my life. Presently, I have a group of friends I met in high school, college, and the workplace. We have developed a special bond, but even so, we don't talk every day. When we see each other, we spend great quality time, laugh, joke, and really catch up, but there's always a distance. I've come to understand that it is because I've internalized that nothing is permanent and everything changes.

All relationships change. People don't stay; they perish and move on as life moves on. The only thing permanent is change. So the sooner you accept change, the less disappointment you will experience. Disappointment comes from expectation and possessiveness. If we don't expect things to be permanent, we wouldn't be so devastated when we have to let them go. This is especially true with material things – I mean, I've lost everything multiple times already – furniture, homes, vehicles; it doesn't even make sense to get attached to anything anymore. I would say that I'm mostly attached to my loved ones, especially my children, and if anything bad ever happens to them, I'd be absolutely destroyed.

However, I think that it's important that we do not claim things as our possessions; they're not our kids. My children are the beings I've created to lead on the best path possible, so it's not my job to possess them or feel like they can never go anywhere. They will go somewhere, and eventually, they will move, and I may experience brief loneliness. Then, I'll learn to appreciate their children and be able to spread more love and information. Possessing things and people doesn't seem to lead to much else but eventual misery. We have to learn to be whole with who we are, remembering that we came onto the planet alone. I think it's really important to appreciate who you are once everything is stripped away and learn to be content and pleased with what you have when there is nothing else.

I don't have any siblings; my mom was almost always working when I was growing up, and my father wasn't usually present. Over the years, I've become aware of my resistance to control-based methods of guidance. People that are close to you might have a hard time supporting whatever you're doing because they're used to being told what to do rather than being allowed to learn life for themselves. My grandmother Alice also had a really hands-off approach to how she raised me, especially when I got to high school.

As a result of how she raised me, I've learned to experience things for myself, and I gained a great depth of knowledge. The experience has helped shape me into someone who doesn't think or behave like most others I meet. Until recently, I never realized that my thought process and behavior were much different than some people who may have had family members offering them advice or suggestions or telling them what to do in terms of careers, relationships, or schooling. I never had those experiences, and it is normal for me to discover life on my own and make decisions on my own terms. I'm not saying that one way is better than the other, just that they are significantly different. It can cause many levels of disharmony when these types of differences aren't recognized and accounted for in an environment.

I don't believe that people should necessarily change the essence of who they are to suit someone else's expectations. Still, there has to be a recognition of the differences in honor of diversity to foster true harmony. If I'm not in alignment with someone, and we don't recognize that it's because of our different backgrounds and life experiences, then we may never really figure out a way to work together and harmonize. Only until those differences are recognized and learned from, and even brought to a balance, are we able to effectively work together by navigating those beautiful nuances that make us more seemingly individual.

The most beautiful tapestries have multiple colors and patterns, different textures, and various hues. There is so much beauty in diversity, and there's no need for us to be homogenous. I appreciate that there needs to be a consideration if you find yourself at odds with someone else, who may be very well-intentioned, but they have a totally different perspective because their life was shaped through an alternate paradigm. Not everyone is necessarily a hater or trying to bring you down, but some people can't get behind something they don't understand. I recognize that it's hard for people to support something when they can't even wrap their minds around it.

Hopefully, through this text, you can find a way to wrap your minds around the people that you haven't yet been able to understand. Maybe their childhood was just totally different than yours, and their life experiences landed them somewhere else with a different mindset and a different set of roles, so they look at life differently, and that is valuable.

Principle 6: Shifting to a Mindset of Abundance

One of the most beautiful things about elevating beyond this scarcity mindset is realizing that it is okay to root for other people, that life is not a competition. Really, we can all win – there are enough seats at the table. If you find out that there are not enough seats when you get there, you can build your own tables. There is more than enough space and opportunity. Who said someone else's table was better?

"A scarcity mindset is **when you are so obsessed with a lack of something** — usually time or money — that you can't seem to focus on anything else, no matter how hard you try. Your brain is too busy thinking about something you don't have. It **makes impulse control harder**. The decision-making part of your brain also controls impulses."[12]

"**Scarcity mentality** refers to people seeing life as a finite pie, so that if one person takes a big piece, that leaves less for everyone else."[13] Sometimes this mindset tricks us into thinking that it has to be me or someone else, that only one of us can make it, and if somebody thinks of or executes something first, then all the ideas are taken. However, ideas are abundant. How many ketchup brands do you see? How many bread brands do you see? How many different brands of cars in various makes and models do you see? "A scarcity mindset is **an attitude which limits creativity and confines people to thinking small about their personal finances**. This fixed scarcity mindset will make you believe that you do not have enough, you will never have enough, and there is very little you can do about it."[14]

Just do your best, encourage other people, and do not be a hater. Always give back, pay it forward, and mentor others. Things will work in your favor when you do the right thing. We do not have to only compete with each other; we can root for each other too. We do not have to exist as each other's competition unless it is healthy competition. It is great to encourage each other. Iron sharpens iron. We can encourage each other to build on our skills and engage in friendly competition, wage bets, and things of that sort. Nevertheless, do not try to tear someone else down, especially someone from your own community. Together, we can transcend these conditions that we experience as a collective; it is possible, but the scarcity mindset and combative energy do not do us any favors.

"In a 2017 experiment, researchers found that simply thinking about an expensive car repair bill significantly worsened the cognitive performance of low-income individuals. These same researchers also studied sugarcane farmers in India, who make the majority of their annual income all at once. At harvest time, the farmers quickly go from poor to relatively rich. The farmers performed much worse on cognitive tests before the harvest when poor than after, despite controlling for stress and other factors. The researchers concluded that poverty "imposes a cognitive load and impedes cognitive capacity" and that these effects are equivalent to losing roughly 13 IQ points — comparable to missing out on a full night of sleep.

Scarcity mindset: a mental shift due to the perception of scarce resources. Our brains have limited bandwidth, so any attention afforded to one immediate problem cannot be used somewhere else. The link between poverty and poor health is well-established. Chronic stress, often the result of constant financial worries, puts millions of [people] at increased risk for a litany of preventable illnesses like heart disease, depression, weight gain, and more. Child poverty can impact brain development, which may lead to mood disorders such as depression and substance abuse later in life. In the United States, children in poverty have lower standardized test scores, are more likely to drop out of school, and are less likely to go to college. When we feel that money and goods are scarce, we start to think of our neighbors and fellow citizens as competitors rather than teammates united by our shared humanity. We have more than enough food, water, shelter, and other goods to meet everyone's basic needs. Scarcity is dead — technology killed it decades ago. The scarcity that remains is a result of poor allocation of resources, not a lack of resources."[15]

"While scarcity focuses on what we don't have, abundant thinking is **an attitude and mindset that focuses on what we do have**. It allows us to see possibility rather than limits and can shift our perspective. An abundance mindset refers **to the paradigm that there is plenty out there for everybody**."[16] It was always intended for us to live this life abundantly. We have been deceived into mindsets that have allowed us to willingly surrender that inheritance to the opposition. "'Abundant life" refers **to life in its abounding fullness of joy and strength for spirit, soul and body**.

"Abundant life" signifies a contrast to feelings of lack, emptiness, and dissatisfaction, and such feelings may motivate a person to seek for the meaning of life and a change in their life."[17]

Principle 7: Support Other People

At Young, Black, & Hustling, we promoted other people's brands fully on social media. We still operate the social network where members sign up at YBHonline.com or YoungBlackHustling.com to share their pictures, videos, and music. They are able to post blogs, discuss topics in the forum, and create groups & events. Each member has their own profile and can chat with other members; the social network was most active in 2013 and 2014. During that time we also ran events where artists came to perform from all over the Mid-Atlantic area, New York, Philadelphia, DC, Virginia, Jersey, Delaware, and Maryland. There would be various types of vendors: fashion designers, jewelers, authors, body care, culinary artists, bakers, and more. We all worked together under the same roof and celebrated art, business, and culture.

YBH's 2014 Anniversary Weekend was one of the best times I have ever had in my life. We started with a networking mixer party on Friday for those who had just arrived in Philadelphia. On Saturday, we had a large Black Wall Street mass vending event. It was like a pop-up mall but with a vast assortment of businesses, and hot food was sold from the kitchen for the entire day. We also had our first Live Artists Showcase that evening, and so much love, support, and positive energy were shared. The vibes were so hype and amazing. On Sunday, the final day, we had the Anniversary Business Bruncheon, where we honored multiple entrepreneurs and artists throughout the area and an NFL player who had been doing amazing things in the Philadelphia community. Through these events, many people were able to get awareness of Young, Black, & Hustling. Since that time, it has been a joy to see so many similar organizations blossom. We have not been as active as we were back then, but it's amazing to see that seeds sprouted and cooperative economic consciousness emerged where people just want to uplift each other. We should spend our time supporting each other, spend our money on each other, moving as a collective, building better worlds together, and leaving something great for our children.

To be in those spaces and to have those experiences is monumental, and I am even happier that I could make it happen with my family. My partner and I met at his catering facility and event space in the Germantown area in Philadelphia, and that is where we hosted the majority of our events. In addition, the lifestyle that we were building, our mini-empire, was a positive example being set within our community. Over the years he's taught me so many things. One thing that I always remember when I think about our relationship and our family is that *Black Love is Revolutionary*.

Principle 8: Visibility Builds Belief

Many people like to see people who have stayed together and worked through whatever kind of challenges they may have. I believe that we are a testimony of how it is to travel from continent to continent and work through financial struggles with the failure and birthing of new businesses. I think that we are an example of how to put down roots in a foreign land and give birth to children at home and work through the process of citizenship, shaping new worlds together.

Visibility matters. Tangible examples matter, and family structures do matter. "When people are able to see something represented, they are better able to understand and grasp who those people are, and this creates an important shift in the social consciousness to include people from a range of different backgrounds. Another crucial piece to consider is that when people see representations of themselves in the media, this can foster a great sense of affirmation of their identity. Feeling affirmed with one's own sense of self can boost positive feelings of self-worth, which is quite different than feeling as if you are wrong or bad for being who you are."[18]

There are many different types of families, and what's most important is when they work together, build together and love each other. We should allow children to see humans loving each other and let them know that love is their birthright. Real Love is possible, and they deserve to know that they are secure and loved.

Self-esteem, self-love, and self-care are of the utmost importance. "Self-esteem is an individual's subjective evaluation of their own worth. Self-esteem encompasses beliefs about oneself (for example, 'I am unloved,' 'I am worthy') as well as emotional states, such as triumph, despair, pride, and shame."

"The self-concept is what we think about the self; self-esteem, is the positive or negative evaluations of the self, as in how we feel about it." [19]The world seems to be evolving to the point where a critical mass of people believes that a lot of the darkness on this planet can be eradicated as more of us adopt concepts like self-love and self-care.

As we begin to release self-doubt and shame, we embrace community and start to love and genuinely care for one another. It is so easy to get a mindset of separation when we are communicating primarily through cellular devices. The same technology that allows us to gather so much knowledge and become aware of the things that are happening around us can be the same thing that divides us. We cannot continue perishing from a lack of knowledge in the age of information.

Even as I communicate with this device right now to transmit this message, I am not speaking to anyone face-to-face. I cannot physically see you, the reader, but I hope that you are getting the message. I am staring into a black mirror, and therefore, it is a conduit that I can use for all of our benefits. However, it can also be used to develop self-destructive habits and behaviors, like comparing ourselves to other people and causing us to develop feelings of inadequacy and depression. It can also be used to fuel division within relationships and cause contention within friendships and family. So, we have to be conscious of the way we are using these tools of technology.

We have to be just as conscious as we are in the way we use money, because that is also a tool. Money can be used for evil and can be used for the greater good. Technology can be used for evil, and it can be used for extreme wickedness. It is all in the choice of the controller who possesses it. What power are you putting into technology, and what energy are you allowing to flow through it? What are you attracting, and what are you creating?

Principle 9: Focus on Your Own Path

If you are in a relay race, and you are being passed the baton, the only thing you are focused on is grabbing that baton and taking off. You stay in your lane, and when it is time, you take off as fast as possible. You make as efficient a handoff to the next person as possible. You do not have time to look from lane to lane and see what everybody else is doing. You have to stay focused on your reception and your handoff, how you take the baton and how you deliver it, how you receive it, and how you pass it on. That is life.

Stay focused on your path. Stay in your lane! When you are looking from lane to lane, you get distracted trying to figure out what everyone else is doing, and you are liable to make comparisons. If you compare your race to others, you cannot possibly run your race efficiently. You have to stay in your lane; it is cliché, but it could not be more accurate. Do you want to pass your children a legacy of comparison or one of strength, pride, and confidence? Stand up straight, firmly planted, stand up strong, and hold your head high. Be proud of the person you are becoming. Raise your children to walk into the room as if they belong there and as if they were expected as honored guests. You walk into a room as if you belong there as if you are highly valued.

We do not need to peek around looking self-conscious, nervous, and being tense. Focus on your lane; you know what you came to do. Enter every situation with a mission and seek to accomplish it. It would be ideal if you could enter every situation with a mission, then you could measure yourself to know if it has been completed or not. You will not stand around awkwardly, trying to compare, looking at people's lives, and focusing on things that do not matter. You will communicate with whom you have to communicate, deliver whatever message you have to deliver, make whatever impact you have to make, and then exit when the time is appropriate.

Principle 10: Always Honor Your Energy

Your presence is the present. You are the secret sauce. If everybody believed that way, then there would be a lot less self-consciousness anxiety going on, a lot less jealousy, and everybody would have the self-esteem required to hold their head high. There wouldn't be a constant yearning for external validation. We could feed ourselves; we could sustain ourselves with our self-love. Self-love does not need codependence; it can sustain itself. Walk into the room as if you belong there. Stay in your lane so you can pass the baton effectively and so that you can handle the future.

Much love to the roots of the world – it is the roots that hold this world together; the fertile ground and indigenous ones. It is those who are from the soil, in the streets, growing daily in resilience and flourishing through hardships. Their struggle fortifies their character and refines them, making diamonds out of coal and sculpting the unbreakable roots of the world – authentically and naturally keeping love as the currency. I love to get into the communities when we travel. I think it's really important if you're roadschooling to learn the local customs of the areas that you're visiting. To me, these are the differences between tourists and travelers. A tourist might want to have a good time dabbling around and pleasing themselves, then go back home, sometimes virtually unchanged.

However, a traveler gets to know each environment. They leave behind the walls of the corporate fortresses and get in touch with the people; they eat the food and enjoy the music. They get to know the customs and try the clothing. Not from the space of appropriation, but rather respect, honor, and learning. Life is all about learning.

Born into a nation of people that have no sovereign land or place to call home (in which we've laid the laws, established educational systems, or have planned structures to feed and protect ourselves), traveling brings an even greater sense of humility because you're very clear that you're on someone else's land and you're a visitor there. You don't need to come with ideas of privilege or exceptionalism, and that you should visit as students. Also, it reminds us that we do not have a definite home anywhere on the planet.

That reminder, and the awareness of this as an international fact, contributes to a certain degree to the post-traumatic stress that has affected us as a collective. Safety, security, shelter, and sustenance are some of the basic things that are requirements for true peace of mind. Without those things, you're always in a survival mindset to some extent. It's really hard to transcend beyond the scarcity and the idea of lack if you're not sure where your meals are coming from or if you're not sure that you have a safe place to raise a family. I do think that those disadvantages will eventually work in our favor.

We, the survivors, have centuries of intentional trauma and subjugation; we were taught to know our "place." Unfortunately, through genetic memory, a lot of those thought forms still manifest in our minds. That time is over. It's now time to reclaim our power and bring along the humility, the resilience, the resourcefulness, the love, and everything that we need to sustain us through these times. A key ingredient is a spirituality that allows us to flourish as survivors, like roses through concrete. Nothing artificial can permanently destroy nature. Nature always prevails.

DIVINE RECIPROCITY.
Chapter V

You Get What You Ask For

When we don't allow ourselves to be desperate, the things that we want can come to us. This means that when we align with our actual goals and get into a state of flow, the things we desire will be drawn to us like a magnet. They will have no choice but to come when we are on the same frequency as our desires. Therefore, desperation causes a disruption because it automatically kicks us out of the flow. We cannot possibly be in alignment if we are in a state of frustration and disbelief.

I have learned that when I act out of desperation, I put myself in a state of misalignment in a way that even worse things came to me out of that desperation. However, when I realized that the things I wanted were considered righteous, I aligned with nature. When I speak of righteousness, I am not speaking religiously; I mean doing the right thing, trying to live right. I am not saying you need to be a vegan or anything like that, though you get my utmost respect for the dietary sacrifice if that is what you choose. Nevertheless, I will say that we should be more conscious of the amount of time we spend with and care for all that is of nature.

The lack of desperation and the acceptance that comes when you enter a state of flow causes you to align with your goals and your visions. It is as if you are relaxing and accepting the reality of what you are calling for; you are expecting its arrival. Therefore, you are applying the behavior that will make it come to you faster, not making choices that could potentially put your vision at risk. Desperation is actually a negative state of being cultivated from a sense of fear and disbelief. You are not accepting that it is already coming to you, so you feel like you have to take matters into your own hands no matter what it takes.

Instead of building positive karma that magnetizes your goals and your visions to you, you are repelling them by applying resistance through the doubt. It is very normal because most people are constantly subject to experience multiple layers of negative "self-talk." Therefore, they often repeat negative thoughts and doubts planted into their subconscious mind. That is not who we are; it is a cumulative voice of those who have programmed us.

Doubt is submitting to those negative thoughts, allowing them to consume you and cause you to act in desperate ways. Desperation does not accomplish goals; it is perseverance that accomplishes goals. In addition to perseverance, there is also consistency, alignment, and cultivating a thought in a specific direction with your circle because when two or three are gathered, the effects will be compounded. I had to learn this lesson by going to jail when I tried to force situations that were already being taken care of because my lack of faith said I needed to take everything into my own hands.

As painful as they can often be, I've learned that consequences are blessings; they are a form of divine correction. Literally, if you don't die from them, there is always a lesson to be learned. Even if you do die, someone else will benefit from the lesson – we are all connected. Without consequences, life would be a constant simulation of pleasantries; therefore, there would be no level of relativity to let us know when to appreciate its joy: the Yin and the Yang. Bad things must happen sometimes; we all begin as fools on some level. We learn, grow, and develop ourselves through the innerstanding of the consequences of our actions. In sequence, a consequence is a reaction to our actions, though not always immediate. This is why making the right decisions is crucial. They may not directly impact us, but they can eventually affect our downlines.

> "For every action (in nature), there is an equal and opposite reaction." (Newton's Third Law of Motion)[20]

Fact of Life: No actions can be taken without setting in motion another set of reactions. Not a thing is independent of itself. Everything is connected, and there will always be ripple effects.

The third law means that all forces are *interactions* between different bodies, or different regions within one body, and thus that there is no such thing as a force that is not accompanied by an equal and opposite force. In some situations, the magnitude and direction of the forces are determined entirely by one of the two bodies, say Body *A*; the force exerted by Body *A* on Body *B* is called the "action", and the force exerted by Body *B* on Body *A* is called the "reaction". This law is sometimes referred to as the *action-reaction law*.[21]

Outside of our linear human way of thinking, consequences occur immediately. While they may be perceived as late or delayed, they are set in motion the moment we conceptualize the thought of an action. If we control our thoughts, then we control the reactions.

> "Choices made, whether bad or good, follow you forever and affect everyone in their path one way or another." (J.E.B. Spredemann) An Unforgivable Secret[22]

Every single choice that's made makes an impression on all future potentials. We can make a decision that puts us on the path to greatness, or we can make a decision that lands us on a path to absolute devastation. The choice is always ours.

I decided to learn taekwondo to maintain my strength and endurance. Usually, I prefer to exercise through boxing (likely a Philly thing), but taekwondo was immediately available, and I've always wanted to be a low-key ninja. As it turns out, I've been enjoying this new activity very much. Every day I choose to voluntarily enhance my body because I know it will lead to a better future for myself and my family. Not only does it build practical skills – it makes it so I can be the most effective mother and businesswoman for as long as possible. It is not as much about vanity or weight loss as I love to enjoy many comfortable and quality meals from all over the world; it is more about longevity and impact. These choices, investments, and sacrifices are of the utmost importance and should be placed relatively high on our list of priorities.

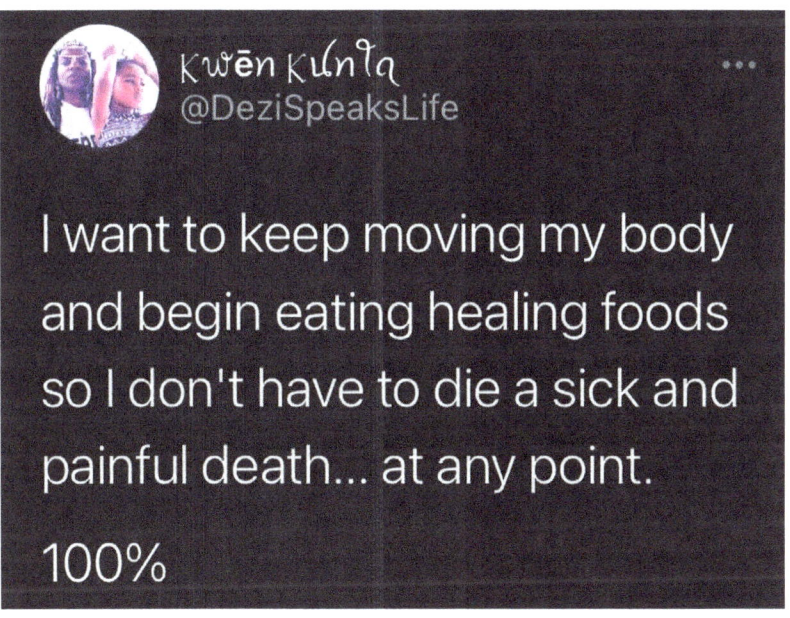

Karma (/ˈkɑːrmə/; Sanskrit: कर्म, IPA: [ˈkɐɽmɐ]; Pali: *kamma*) **means** *action, work, or deed.* **The term also refers to the spiritual principle of cause and effect, often descriptively called the principle of karma, wherein intent and actions of an individual (cause) influence the future of that individual (effect): good intent and good deeds contribute to good karma and happier rebirths, while bad intent and bad deeds contribute to bad karma and bad rebirths.[23]**

> "How people treat you is their karma; how you react is yours".[24]
> (Wayne Dyer)

Learning to be a lotus in muddy waters. Allowing nothing and no one to knock you off your Square. Being confident that you're creating the best karma for yourself. Knowing that whatever comes to us is a reaction to what we called forth earlier.

> "Problems or successes, they all are the results of our own actions. Karma. The philosophy of action is that no one else is the giver of peace or happiness. One's own karma, one's own actions are responsible to come to bring either happiness or success or whatever."[25] (Maharishi Mahesh Yogi)

The best thing about karma is that it's always changing. You don't have to waste time feeling bad about the past when you can consciously make choices to build better karma. After you're aware of this, the only way not to create better karma is by intentionally choosing not to do it. That's the beauty of personal development, you can slow it down, but the direction keeps moving forward.

> "I would never disrespect any man, woman, chick or child out there. We're all the same. What goes around comes around, and karma kicks us all in the butt in the end of the day."[26] (Angie Stone)

Too often, we focus on the individuality that keeps us separate, when truly, we are all connected. What we do to others will impact us in one way or another. There is no real separation, only delusion.

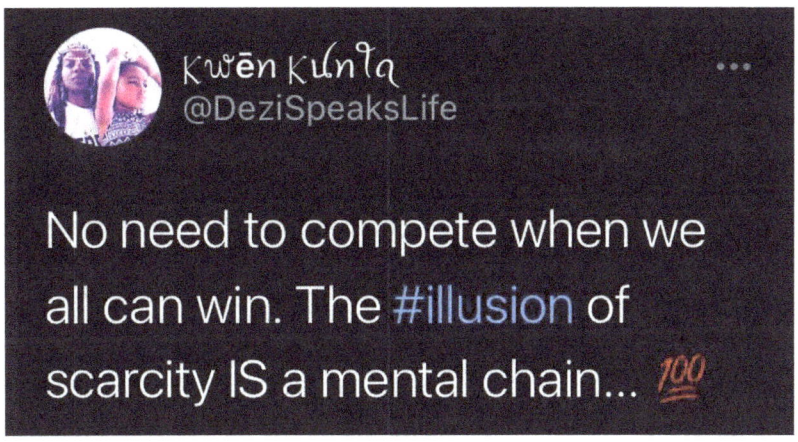

Kwēn Kunta
@DeziSpeaksLife

No need to compete when we all can win. The #illusion of scarcity IS a mental chain... 💯

"Therefore shall they eat of the fruit of their own way, and be filled with their own devices." Proverbs 1:31[27] King James Bible

Sometimes you see a tree in the winter or in its youth and are unable to identify it. Then later, you discover the type of tree it is when it develops and bears its fruits. These fruits can be anything from delicious to poisonous. We cultivate and grow our own gardens, and they are the gardens that we will eat from.

"There are in nature neither rewards nor punishments — there are consequences."[28] (Robert G. Ingersoll) The Christian Religion: An Enquiry

I like the idea of rewards and positive reinforcement, yet typically, the idea concentrates on the forces at work externally. When we call for our own consequences and blessings, we take ownership of our circumstances.

"Do not be deceived, God is not mocked; for whatever a man sows, that he will also reap. For he who sows to the flesh will of the flesh reap corruption, but he who sows to the Spirit will of the Spirit reap everlasting life." Galatians 6:7-8[29] The New King James Version

Sometimes we are too busy to help someone in need. Maybe we don't have enough cash or the ability to share our resources. Do remember that there may be a time when we are in need also. The karma that we have already created is what will be there to face us. It is not our responsibility to judge why someone else needs something; it is our responsibility to serve humanity and be a benefit to this planet. We have been created to serve the creation. We are not above the law; we are from the law. So even if we don't believe the law, the law still applies.

> "Tse-kung asked, 'Is there one word that can serve as a principle of conduct for life?' Confucius replied, 'It is the word 'shu' -- reciprocity. Do not impose on others what you yourself do not desire.'"[30] (Doctrine of the Mean 13.3)

Some of you might think the above principle is pretty basic. My mother used to say often, "Do unto others as you would have others do unto you." The Golden Rule – something that seems simple as science. Yet as we grow, we notice that a whole lot is done to others without, seemingly, a thought of reciprocity. Maybe it's already accepted or totally neglected. It's always a great time to remember that we will attract the same energy we give to others. I think you may as well make it good!

> And whatever strikes you of disaster – it is for what your hands have earned; And He pardons much. [31] (Quran Surah Shura 42:30)

I love how many of the world's religions repeat the same ancient truths. Given their consistency and even their accuracy in science allows me to be confident that they must actually be true. Not just that, but by the way the principles apply to our personal lives, to my personal life. I have recognized my karma so many times that I now consciously and selfishly behave in a way to call the best possible experiences into my future. The real beauty of life is found in balance.

Kwēn Kúnla
@DeziSpeaksLife

The way we treat beings we believe are powerless is the truest testament to our character.

> The one who loves all intensely begins perceiving in all living beings a part of himself. He becomes a lover of all, a part and parcel of the Universal Joy. He flows with the stream of happiness, and is enriched by each soul.[32] (Yajur Veda)

The Journey. I've learned to respect each stage of my journey and innerstand that this life school is intended to graduate us to the "next level" of consciousness or awareness. Tests and trials, risks and rewards, good times and bad times, all help us to develop into greater beings. We were not created to stay the same but to grow mentally, physically, and spiritually. I consider it an honor to know that our Creator is witnessing, sharing, and guiding my growth.

> O seeker, know the true nature of your soul, and identify yourself with it completely. O Lord, (may we attain) the everlasting consciousness of Supreme Light and Joy. May we resolve to dedicate our life to the service of humankind, and uplift them to Divinity.[33] (Yajur Veda)

We can live hell on this earth, or we can make it our paradise. Although we cannot control what has happened to us in our youth, it is our responsibility to seek healing. The healing will take us to higher levels of existence and begin to disintegrate generational curses. We do this not only for ourselves but for our families' futures, and some may even say that we heal those who have passed as well.

"Success is a consequence and must not be a goal."[34] **(Gustave Flaubert)**

Sometimes we can find ourselves feeling tired and drained from living our day-to-day lives. We think we might be doing too much or moving around too much, and sometimes, we are. However, in many instances, we are simply not doing things that fuel our passion. Passion revives our energy. Our life force energy can be drained away when we do things that seem mundane simply out of necessity, survival, or duty. It is normal to feel very tired of these activities. You get tired of the rituals, the schedules, and doing things that do not serve you on any level beyond the financial.

You have found your purpose when you begin to do things that bring you joy, and not because you are on vacation or seeking thrills, but because you're finally living in your purpose. This is when you are doing something every day that you are passionate about; passion is very important. When they hear the word passion, I know some people think that you are speaking in a sexual sense or something romantic. Have you ever heard a person give a speech, and their words sound monotonous, and you do not actually walk away with the full effect of their message? It is because their tone lacks passion, and it seems as if they may have even been reading the words written by somebody else. They may even seem to lack sincerity. When you hear someone speak and it is full of passion, it is as if the words are coming directly from their heart. You can see the excitement not only in their body language but also in their eyes. It is like a spark, a divine spark.

'"What was that? An Exhibition? We need emotional content. Now try again!'

What did Bruce Lee mean by 'Emotional Content?' He was describing the feeling of being totally present in your body and connected to your own life force. A spiritual life force that is the energy of creation. This force helps you become a human being from moment to moment. When you are creating emotional content, you are creating in awareness, openness and receptivity to everything around you. You are in a state of relating to your surroundings. You are not in isolation—you are connected."[35]

"If you feel like there's something out there that you're supposed to be doing, if you have a passion for it, then stop wishing and just do it."[36] (Wanda Sykes)

I once read that within some of us, or even all of us dwells a passion gene that could be activated. Something that, once triggered, can ensure that everything we frequently do becomes magnetized towards greatness. "Passion, then, might develop over time from a genetic advantage that gives rise to a superior physical or intellectual skill, which moreover provides an individual with a consistent source of gratification. In turn, this sense of satisfaction reinforces the individual's willingness to continue to develop his or her skill. The combination of compulsive practice and passion leads to mastery and exceptional achievement. The first thing they found was a greater dopaminergic activity in areas of the brain associated with reward and motivation for participants who were more willing to work hard in exchange for greater rewards. Secondly, they found an inverse relationship between dopamine activity and the insula, a part of the brain that has been associated with laziness. This means, in short, that labor becomes love for some. For others, it evoked a stale and lackluster sense of motivation."[37]

When we walk with purpose and live out our passions, it is hard to fall into a deep depression.

It is interesting how much the diagnosis of depression has soared over the past few decades. Even though people have been dealing with hardships since the beginning of time, we have come to an age where we have all the luxuries and conveniences of a financial system; we live in these fancy boxes, work in stable jobs, and possess pleasing titles. Everybody wants an important label to call themselves. Everybody has the potential to be "somebody" yet, anxiety, depression, and mental illness of all sorts are at an all-time high. Could there possibly be some correlation with the fact that we are just not living out our natural-born purposes while subject to existence under constructs such as scarcity and the dependence on money for survival?

I believe earth serves as a school for souls. We all came here with some intention, a very specific intention that we may not remember after we arrived as infants through the portal of our mother's womb. However, that does not negate the fact that we all have a purpose, and we are predestined for some level of greatness, without exception. Some souls see it through, they are able to make it happen while they are still here on this planet, but many souls do not. I believe we arrive at a level of disillusionment somewhere in the middle of life when we realize that we've been wasting so much time doing what we've been told by other humans, whether it's our parents, teachers, or religious leaders. In addition, we are not doing anything that furthers our life goals and purpose. We have been distracted and have been wasting our youth and our life force energy. We have been spending the bit of life that we have left in our bodies furthering the goals of others and enhancing the agendas of other entities. That can undoubtedly bring high levels of stress, depression, anxiety, and all sorts of mental illness.

How does it feel to realize that you have been wasting your life? What can you do about that? Is the solution only a decision away? Can we simply decide to make a plan to delve into the deepest recesses of our minds and remember what it is that we truly love? What sparked the most excitement in our childhood? How hard can it be to remember what it is that brought us the most joy? It could even be a hobby.

I read somewhere recently that everyone should have five hobbies. One that brings them money, a hobby that keeps them fit, a hobby that helps them develop in a spiritual or emotional sense, a hobby that allows them to create, and a hobby to simply experience joy. These hobbies, when practiced effectively and strategized appropriately, can reap significant financial gains. It is possible that with consistent action and the elimination of indecision, you can live the life of your dreams.

> **"Every great dream begins with a dreamer. Always remember, you have within you the strength, the patience, and the passion to reach for the stars, to change the world."**[36] **(Harriet Tubman)**

Too often, we are trained to believe that greatness is on the other side of death. That we have to die in order to experience a sense of heaven or a sense that we have made it. Many people here on earth are living out their wildest goals and dreams because they decided they wanted to or were able to through inheritance. It is important that we work at a higher level of decisive action toward our tangible goals. Please note that I said tangible and not realistic, as some people think that "realistic" means you have to think small or remain inside the box. They think that way because, for them, most things outside of their box are considered fantasy. Accomplishments are easier to relate to if you have seen someone familiar do it, especially someone who is a reflection of you. It could be someone who is no smarter, or more brilliant; they may not even be spectacularly talented. These people probably do believe in themselves a lot more than you do; they might have been encouraged more than you have or have a higher level of self-determination than you possess. Those factors lead to personal greatness in the attainment of life goals. Moreover, if those attributes are the only differences, they can be easily developed. They are just one action-based decision away.

You have to decide to develop self-esteem and self-determination; you already possess the intelligence, you are not an imposter. We eliminate the Imposter Syndrome by building on our skills. Know that if someone else can do it, you can do it as well. No one is better than you are. We have been trained to idolize and externalize confidence to celebrities and all sorts of people who have become famous for various reasons. However, in most cases, they are not anymore capable than you are. They have the same number of hours in the day as you do. They are also humans who have come into this world through their mother's womb portal with a purpose, and for whatever reason, they may or may not be living out that purpose. Maybe someone made it easy for them, and that is okay. Let that not affect your story.

The work you put in to get out of the situation you no longer want to be in will be a part of your victory. This struggle will build resilience that helps you keep on and let you hold on because you know what it's like not to have your dream. The struggle that you experience, the dedication and sacrifice you made will be the thing that allows you to keep what it is that you desire; you will not waste it. You will appreciate it because you did the work for it, and therefore, it will happen. It is only a sequential decision away.

"The future belongs to those who prepare for it today."[38] **(Malcolm X)**

86

Chapter VI
LESSONS.

Learning From the Outcomes of Life's Tests

*B*efore arriving at Cook County Jail, I discovered I was being charged with two felonies (a Class X, 6-30 years, and a Class 1, 4-15 years). The Class X included no chances of probation.

I remember people saying you have to appear to be crazy when you go to jail. Maybe that was just in movies, but I wasn't taking any chances. On the bus transporting us from the courthouse to the county jail, I was pulled into a conversation with two other young women. They seemed to be a couple and were quite comfortable as they expressed their familiarity with the situation. It was during this conversation that I decided to tell other inmates that I was locked up for feeding people to my pitbull, when asked. While I did have a pitbull, he was the sweetest creature you'd ever meet. I'm not sure anyone ever believed that wild story, but everyone who heard it seemed amused. I made a fair number of friends during my stay at Cook County, and I keep up with some women till this day. The lesson I learned in this situation was that no matter how difficult the task, things can still work in your favor if you keep an open attitude and corresponding energy.

Even as I write this, I'm speaking to myself and encouraging myself. Lessons are life's teaching tools. I learned, pretty long ago, that tests are not passed until the lessons get learned. Even though I'm reminded of this often, I'm grateful to have the innerstanding and faith. I've watched people go through the same things day after day, year after year, and fail to learn lessons from them. I've learned that people have to learn their lessons on their own time, even though proper guidance and examples can point them in the right direction. We cannot rush others to truly embrace their lessons, even though I often try to rush myself. I've learned that we all have our own life's path, and I want to learn my lessons as quickly as possible to graduate to each new level while there is still vitality and breath in this living body. Through this, hopefully, my children can learn from my lessons, and we can offer worthy contributions to human evolution.

"Good judgment comes from experience, and experience comes from bad judgment."[39] **(Rita Mae Brown)**

While I was in jail awaiting my fate, I decided to fast and read the Bible with a couple of my new friends. We started at Matthew and concluded with Mark. During those three days, I became aware of the pattern of those who had court dates nearby. The day before, they would seem very positive and behave like a newly reformed person, then when they came back with a continuance (which happened most often) or even worse news, they would come back angrier or more defeated than when they first arrived. Few of the lessons of the situation were being learned or even recognized. I clearly noticed myself changing into a different and more dangerous person. Through the realization and acceptance of the lesson, that I would not get through this situation until I realized what character flaws landed me there, I believe I was blessed with the opportunity of early release. It is our responsibility to learn and graduate or surrender to forces that will have us repeat the same lessons over and over and over. Eventually, the lessons will be learned.

> "It can be said that wisdom, in turn, acts properly upon that knowledge. Wisdom is the fitting application of knowledge. Knowledge understands the light has turned red; wisdom applies the brakes. Knowledge sees the quicksand; wisdom walks around it"[40] - quote taken from the blog "What is the difference between wisdom and knowledge?" by Paul Koptak

So many times, we possess life-changing information but, for some reason, are slow to use it to our benefit. We might see leaders endeavoring to teach others how to be free, healthy, and courageous, without acting on those same teachings themselves. There are instances when we become complacent in our situations that we might not desire to rid ourselves of our chains. Mental bondage can become comfortable, dependable, and familiar. Wisdom is not a cheap party favor; it develops through life's toughest lessons, and it requires practical application of knowledge and discovered understanding.

Wisdom is found in the application of gathered knowledge and awareness. It's not enough that we know something; it's more important that we use it practically. It's false wisdom to have knowledge of something then consciously choose not to apply it. At that point, what sounds like wisdom is not true wisdom but false wisdom. Wisdom is recognized when it is used with discernment and forethought.

Depending on where you come from, there are so many tricks set up for you along the way. Life truly has to be navigated through a spiritual lens. From the time we're born, we're assigned a situation. When some people first entered elementary school, they were harassed by over-sexualization, negative influences, and peer pressure. So many beautiful souls have fallen into these traps over the years. It's a miracle any of us survive till adulthood, for the lessons in wisdom begin too early. We became super-natural wildflowers where our growth could no longer be contained.

KNOWLEDGE   WISDOM

"The dictionary defines wisdom as 'the ability to discern or judge what is true, right, or lasting.' Knowledge, on the other hand, is 'information gained through experience, reasoning, or acquaintance.' Knowledge can exist without wisdom, but not the other way around. One can be knowledgeable without being wise. Knowledge is knowing how to use a gun; wisdom is knowing when to use it and when to keep it holstered." [40]- quote taken from the blog "What is the difference between wisdom and knowledge?" by Paul Koptak

Wear your scars proudly! *Authenticity, Honesty, Relatability, and Integrity. When you know you've done your best, be proud of yourself. If you have not done your best, begin doing your best. Be proud of who you are. Honor the journey that has brought you to this point because it's like your celestial fingerprint. No one ever has or ever shall walk your path. From start to finish, it is the most real thing that makes you unique. Let's grab our best walking shoes!*

Now, I must acknowledge that my way of thinking comes from the level of confidence instilled by most of my elders. Most of them allowed me to believe that I could be anything I decided to be and accomplish whatever I set my mind to. Even after constant and public failure, my mom is still my biggest cheerleader. The manner in which we speak to children has a tremendous impact on the adults they ultimately become. As a result of their belief in me, I am not afraid to try different things. The negative self-talk and programming often provided by guardians can handicap people until the day they die. This cannot be ignored and should be addressed with the utmost immediacy.

Sometimes, I am reminded of this when raising my voice or becoming overly frustrated with the little ones. Children deserve patience, respect, and kindness. The traumas from my past should never negatively impact the futures of my children. They are the humans in our care; in most cases, we created them, and in all cases, it is our responsibility that they grow to become balanced people who can contribute to their communities. Finally, correcting these cycles can break a generational curse. Isn't this the purpose of evolution?

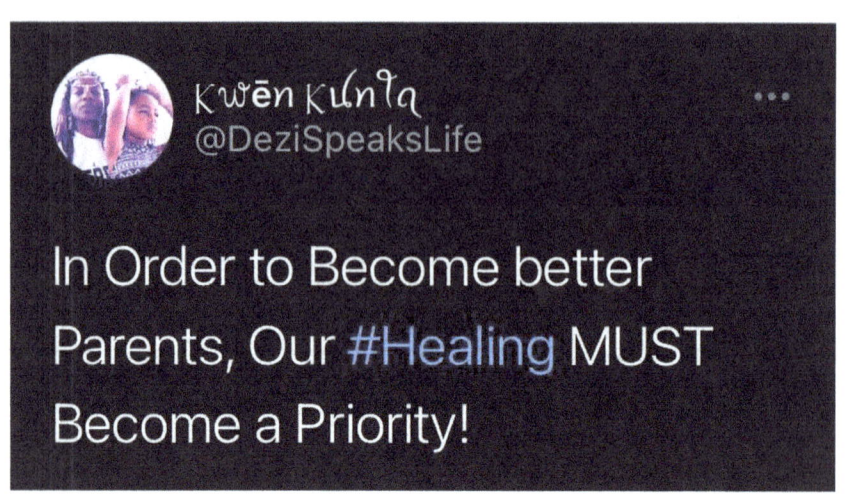

Kᴡēn Kᴜ́nⁱᵃ
@DeziSpeaksLife

In Order to Become better Parents, Our #Healing MUST Become a Priority!

"I am not someone who is ashamed of my past. I'm actually really proud. I know I made a lot of mistakes, but they, in turn, were my life lessons." [41] **(Drew Barrymore)**

Gratefully, I can say that I'm living life with very few regrets. The goal is not to avoid all regret, but to not die full of them. There are many mistakes I wish I could take back, actions that I neglected to take, and times that I was far too selfish. When I become aware of something that I am doing wrong, I try to face it and begin to correct it. We all miss the mark; God knows I do. Awareness is the gift that leads to continued growth. It will lead us to a true blossoming of our souls, to our paths of purpose and passion in authenticity. Bliss will magnetize abundance, and flow will take you over to new heights. Consistency will be your anchor, and gratitude will be your guide.

One lesson that I'm still learning, for sure, is to fully appreciate the time that we have with our loved ones. Visit with your elders, quickly return missed phone calls, and thoroughly engage in the conversations you're still able to have. Even though your elders may be familiar, they have a wealth of knowledge they're usually more than willing to share when asked the right questions. I know I'm not the only person who is tired of losing people without spending the quality time with them that I thought I had left. This is especially relevant right now, during a global health scare and mass tragedies. We should not be losing people in front of our eyes, in our homes, without access to proper medical care. Finances should not be the reason our lives are worth less. Yet, this is where we've found ourselves, in a predicament where loving strongly on each other while building toward self-sustainability is the only practical solution.

What I think I like most about elders is that many of them are so past the opinions of others. Of course, I know there are older but still immature people due to a lack of life experiences or traumas that have delayed them from evolving or growing. However, for the most part, older people seem to be more authentic, more willing to speak their minds, and spend less time trying to put on appearances for external approval. I enjoy having candid conversations with them, and they usually don't mind keeping it real. I really appreciate finding peers who are the same way, mature beyond their years for various reasons, but because they seem like a rarity, I gravitate toward communication with those advanced in years – the golden ones.

Building trustful relationships with other people, especially my peers, might be one of the toughest parts of my healing journey, but lately, I have been learning to get out and be more sociable. I've even been reconnecting with old friends and making plans with them for the future. That's my progress, what about yours? What is it that you need to work on? Do you experience similar issues with trust and the fear of betrayal? To me right now, I believe the fear of betrayal is the most prominent because I have so many business plans in the works. When you're trying to build an empire, you can't afford to surround yourself with weak links or people that can't behave properly and become a cancer to your project or the circle you're creating.

I think it's important that we closely consider the people we keep company with, probably not to the extent of paranoia, but take it as seriously as the food we consume or where we choose to live. Your company can quite literally dictate your future. I also understand the need to create community when you're building a community-based business. Too often, many new executives like to carry everything on their shoulders, but things must be delegated for a business to run efficiently and become sustainable. Responsibilities must be entrusted to trustworthy and competent people, and risks have to be taken to identify those talents. That means I need to be able to put myself out there more frequently and learn to trust people more. Also, I need to understand that many people have similar fears and frustrations about collaborating with others. I need to expand my vibration to attract people who are my tribeswomen and tribesmen who have a similar mindset.

Since privacy is an illusion these days anyway, I'm not quite sure why the idea of surveillance still gets me so paranoid. I know had it not been for surveillance, I would not have lost my freedom. However, in the global age, we are being watched and listened to as our communications are being monitored, whether it be on our cell phones, the laptop that we use to get work done, or the cameras in the stores and around our neighborhoods. So, I always try to behave as if I'm being watched.

However, I think it's very important to trust other humans and beings, be your sensitive self, and sometimes have that safe space in your innermost circle, where you can feel free from judgment. That's what most people that have suffered from PTSD need; they need a place to feel safe. In some communities like where I'm from, PTSD is a widespread and commonly undiagnosed issue, and many people from our communities are suffering from this issue to extreme levels. We watch it play itself out on the daily news, and trauma is something many of us regularly absorb, as frequently as using the restroom. It becomes compounded and possibly permanently ingrained.

We see friends die in front of our faces, rampant drug abuse, and homelessness; we deal with frequent threats of eviction, child and spousal abuse, an absolute absence of safety and peace of mind, and all kinds of things that become the norm for us that are traumatic. We've gotten to the point that we're so accustomed to dealing with it that we don't recognize that it's trauma because it's become normalized. Just because we're used to being abused and misused doesn't mean that we should continue to be abused and misused. Just because we're accustomed to being at the bottom of the barrel and treated like the trashcan of the world does not mean that we should allow ourselves to be in that situation and continue to tolerate it.

Post Traumatic Stress Disorder or PTSD, as much as I hate labels, is the stress that takes place after trauma – daily trauma and constant trauma. It results from the stress of financial issues and various types of conditions dealt with that destroy homes and kill us. I can't personally say that I know anyone from any hood that does not have some level of post-traumatic stress that they are dealing with regularly.

By "hood," I mean anywhere on the planet where the people are marginalized and subjugated to the lowest socioeconomic stations available. It's time for reform and social justice to no longer just be jargon. There needs to be a serious movement to rearrange priorities within the global economic structure because no one can truly be liberated until we are all liberated.

Another lesson I would like to touch on is discerning when to use the words "no" and "yes" appropriately. See, some of us say yes to everything. We run ourselves into the ground, trying to accommodate everyone's requests because we are people pleasers. We want to make sure that everybody likes us and that everybody has something positive to say about us. That is unsustainable and unrealistic. Actually, when you say yes all the time, it shows that you do not value your time. When you are always saying yes to the same person, and you eventually say no, sometimes that person gets upset. They do so because they have grown so accustomed to using your agreeableness that they do not get a chance to truly appreciate your yeses.

Be there for yourself. First and foremost, be loyal to yourself. Your first concern should be how you are doing. Are you okay? If you are not okay, you cannot effectively get any job done for anyone, your family, or even yourself. You will burn yourself out energetically and physically.

On the other hand, some people always say no. These people miss many very exciting opportunities. It is not just about excitement; they also miss many opportunities for personal growth and development. For example, you may be in a situation where someone is offering you a position to travel and blog for a certain amount of money, and you declined the offer because fear has gotten in the way, or you need to be there for family, your job, or because something else that you think may suit you better, or even a relationship. You may be missing out on incredible opportunities that can enrich your life and allow you to build skills and have experiences that totally shift the way you think. These opportunities could put you on a different level financially through meeting people that can open doors for you that you would never have had access to.

Saying "no" out of fear consistently is definitely a huge barrier to success. It is important to find a balance when saying "yes" and saying "no." I would not say "yes" all the time.

However, I certainly will make sure that all of my responses are not "no." I would rather have too many amazing experiences than too few. I would rather leave this planet knowing that I completed as many things as possible than always avoiding something because it seemed inconvenient or the time was never right.

Balance is key. In everything, balance is key; there is no black and white in anything. Even when discussing good and evil, know that good people can commit great evil. In addition, those we call evil can do great things.

Every person on the planet has known someone they love that they would do anything for. I want you to really digest that there is good and bad in everything; there is no total black and white. The God of the Bible is certainly a balanced being, and when we begin to look at life from a non-dualistic point of view, we realize that we can also reach a balance, and it is beneficial. So many times, we want to be perfect and be everything to everybody, especially in this age of social media. We have this idea that perfection is attainable, that other people are more acceptable, but we are inadequate and possess too many flaws. We should instead focus on growing and being the best version of ourselves. When we do things that are not always right, because we will do wrong things, we correct them and continue on our growth path. Sometimes we may be too imprudent and make decisions that are not best for everyone, and sometimes we may be too giving, cruel, or merciful. It is all about balance. The key to life, the purpose of being on this planet, is to help us develop into the highest versions of ourselves so that we can eventually graduate to higher levels of existence.

I do not believe that earth is our final home. I do not believe we came here just to eat, sleep, work, have children, die, repeat; I believe we were created for a greater purpose. The same way children are born into a new world; I believe the same thing with death. When we die, we transition into another state of being. Death is not the end, though we've been heavily programmed to fear it, by intention. So, if you're saying "no" or avoiding situations because you fear death, stop it. On this earth, we are siloed into societies where they place us under high levels of stress and fear because people who are afraid to die can be controlled more easily than people who do not fear death. We are all placed under these programs that focus on the fear of death consistently and continuously. Fear is necessary to maintain the externalization of our confidence and authority.

We will never be able to live our fullest lives if we continue succumbing to that programming. In New Amerykah Part 1, The Healer, Erykah Badu sings, **"You don't have to believe everything you think. We've been programmed, wake up..."** [42] Sometimes our thoughts are our worst enemies. What we think – our mental chains are the things that are keeping us in bondage. Marcus Garvey wrote, **"We are going to emancipate ourselves**

from mental slavery because whilst others might free the body, none but ourselves can free the mind. Mind is your only ruler, sovereign. The man who is not able to develop and use his mind is bound to be the slave of the other man who uses his mind." [43]

Life does not have to be a constant struggle. The chains that are put around us are no longer on our feet and our ankles, no longer around our necks. They have been programmed and transplanted into our minds. It is not particularly a racial, ethnic, or nationality thing anymore and can be witnessed all over this planet. Put on the full armor because wickedness certainly abounds in the high places.

Like mosquitoes, there are indeed entities that sniff out goodness and vulnerability so that they can slowly extract the soul. There are people who have almost everything – those in power and those who fight over the cumulative leftovers, the powerless. The powerlessness does not come solely from the lack of resources. The powerlessness comes out of the fact that we have surrendered our power due to fear. We may even be afraid of our own power subconsciously. We were trained to fear our power and voluntarily relinquish that power into the hands of others who do not have our best interests at heart because if they did, it would not serve their interests of domination. It is time to reclaim our power. This is for those who choose to seek a path to personal sovereignty. To be sovereign means that you are living life on your terms.

It doesn't mean that you are out of control, but that you are fully under self-control. That you are self-disciplined and you make beneficial decisions for yourself. It is not chaos; this is not a conversation for the advocacy of anarchy. It is for liberation, personal power, and understanding that you can control yourself by controlling your thoughts, with the awareness that those thoughts automatically translate into your actions. Your actions automatically translate into habits which become the programs that create your character, while your character determines your entire lifestyle. How we are perceived, how we behave, how we live, how we raise our children, how we interact in a community, and our legacy begins with our thoughts.

Therefore, who can tell me that the initial step of controlling our thoughts is not of the highest importance? Sovereignty and personal freedom begin with controlling our thoughts or carefully crafting and curating the content that we consume that influences our thoughts. You might have to delete half of your "friends" or remove social media altogether. Do you want to be accepted, or do you want to be in control of your life?

When we begin to have thoughts that are not in alignment with the future that we want to have, we can gently redirect our thoughts to more beneficial ones, intentionally feed ourselves more beneficial content, and slowly begin to eliminate non-beneficial content just like someone going on a diet.

If someone had been eating white rice with every meal for the past thirty years, we would not tell them to stop eating it all of a sudden; we would encourage them to lessen the amount that they eat every day and substitute at times with brown rice. We have to work in baby steps in order for change to be impactful. We want to be gentle with ourselves; we do not want to punish ourselves. Personal development is not about punishment but correction.

Self-discipline does not have to be painful. Unless you are currently killing yourself, you do not need to stop something cold turkey. Gradual changes are beneficial, and they are much more sustainable, meaning that they are much more likely to last for your entire life.

Chapter VII
TRANSMUTATION.

Remembering Who You Are

I have often heard that we should try to do things the "right way" – the manner in which goals have been achieved for years by various members of previous generational cohorts. After following such directives, I still did not feel satisfactory. Things were, and still are, changing. I attended networking events, applied for, and gathered at rushes for organizations that I still was not accepted into, no matter how good my grades were or what level of community service I dedicated myself to. Over time, group acceptance no longer intrigued me the way it once did. I did not mind becoming a lone wolf, and I still do not mind walking dark paths by myself. However, I do mind changing who I am to fit into someone else's mold. I never want to feel like I walked on eggshells too much just for my message to be palatable, though I understand that we must know our audience and try to show respect. There are respectful ways to be honest, and we should get to know them because there is no integrity without honesty.

Many rich people are slaves because they cannot be themselves or speak their minds. You can be a high-paid slave, and by slave, I mean controlled by someone else. Your actions are not your own. You cannot say what you want to say. It may not even be about money. Sometimes we are slaves to our reputations. We build up these personas that we believe we must live up to, and the idea of it being stripped away makes us feel like we will not even be a person anymore. The idea of changing with new information or understanding that we are not perfect sometimes makes people deal with identity crises. It is very possible to be a slave to the opinions of others. Personally, I do not wish to be enslaved by anything.

In this composition I try not to mince my words too much, yet understanding that this is a diverse audience, I try to maintain awareness of that. Please excuse me if my words offend you; they are only meant to be genuine. I understand the need to grow in grace and speak more eloquently or to use words that are more easily digestible for people of all backgrounds. That is something that I am learning and growing into, and maybe I will reach it by the time I am fifty years old; perhaps I will not. My ninety-nine-year-old grandma still says what she wants, when she wants, and to whomever she wants without any shame. Maybe that characteristic will not change, but I promise to be my best.

I belong to a large family full of opinionated, big-mouthed, talented women with the brains to match. They can engage with anyone verbally, and I am fairly certain they would prevail, or maybe they have not met their matches. The culture that has been developed through the matriarchs, verbal acuity, and lack of restriction has made it to the point where none of us bite our tongues too often, and sometimes it has been a source of internal strife. Everyone still loves each other and has each other's back, for the most part. I am grateful to come from a long lineage of powerful women on both sides. To know that these women are in my DNA makes me feel honored.

The women who raised me were so strong that I could say I have never seen them abused or mistreated by men. If anything, they took too good care of men; they were solid nurturers. As I have grown older, I think that has a lot to do with what I will and will not tolerate in my life. My maternal grandmother raised eight children with a working, veteran, alcoholic husband, and I've been blessed to witness the results. She pulled the money together, and she bought a house for them. This woman was not formally educated, but she had a potent mind and a compelling determination to watch them succeed. In addition, she planted morals and standards for them that have passed on to multiple generations; she has truly birthed a formidable empire.

I saw my paternal grandmother take care of her sons until she could no longer keep her mind. My mother was the provider in every relationship I have ever seen her in, and I saw her go through some things that I would not want to go through. However, I have never seen anyone put their hands on her or speak to her in ways that I thought were particularly offensive, at least not in my presence. Sometimes, I see peers go through things that I know are the results of their upbringing and what they saw their mothers and fathers go through. It is evident that what we experience as children directly impacts what we allow in our adult lives.

"Researches have concluded that childhood trauma, whether it's because of physical, **emotional, sexual abuse or accidental wise** can raise distress in adulthood relationships. Neglecting the child or constantly criticizing them disrespectfully can induce similar behavior among them when they become adults."[44] We wonder how women go from one abusive relationship to another, or men constantly date women that cheat on them, and yet we are still magnetizing the same situation repeatedly to ourselves. Why are we expecting this behavior? Is it because it has become a norm from childhood? Do we unintentionally attract people that remind us of our parents? I believe we do. I unquestionably recognize that my relationship with my parents has impacted my personal relationships.

"Living through traumatic events may **result in expectations of danger, betrayal, or potential harm within new or old relationships**. Survivors may feel vulnerable and confused about what is safe, and therefore it may be difficult to trust others, even those whom they trusted in the past."[45] "This trauma can also impact a person into adulthood as they experience **feelings of shame and guilt, feeling disconnected and unable to relate to others**, trouble controlling emotions, heightened anxiety and depression, anger."[46]

With that recognition, we can try to cope and make adjustments, but is it possible that some things cannot be changed? We could surrender our power by choosing to believe that some things are what they are, that we'll just have to make lemonade with those lemons and count our blessings. Or learn to understand that "the functions of the amygdala, hippocampus, and the prefrontal cortex that are affected by trauma can be reversed. **The brain is ever-changing and recovery is possible**."[47]

"One fails forward toward success."[48] **(Charles F. Kettering)**

Over the years, I've learned that choosing to do the right thing may not always be the easiest, but it always leads to the best long-term outcomes. I've made so many mistakes as if I'm stumbling through life trying to move forward. Each failure surely brings us closer to the nearest success. I have no doubt that perseverance, backed by the right intentions, will lead us exactly where God meant for us to be – while listening to the quiet voice of wisdom that becomes louder each time we choose to obey it and following the guidance of those with wisdom, that have been divinely introduced into our lives and have already accomplished the goals that we are chasing.

FAILING FORWARD.
Chapter VIII

Allowing mistakes, and corrections, to guide you toward your ultimate purpose.

Keep failing until you succeed. *There is this meme where a man is digging in search of diamonds, and it appears as if he was digging for years. At one point, he decided to quit digging and turn around for home. Then another man showed up and decided to resume the previous man's digging. It turns out that after a few more feet of digging, he discovered a massive diamond mine. Such a bitter-sweet message this image possesses.*

With the right mindset and intention, synced with consistency, things will always work out eventually. Do not doubt yourself or your purpose. Keep going until you make it, then keep going some more. True purpose lasts a lifetime. We should never stop learning and growing.

> **"And we know that in all things God works for the good of those who love him, who have been called according to his purpose."** [49]
> **(Romans 8:28)** New International Version

A calling is a compelling feeling that you know must be satisfied, and if you do not complete it, your soul may begin to die. Imagine that calling aligned with divine purpose. The divine purpose ensures that the endeavor is fulfilled as it has been chosen and directed.

> **"Failure is nature's plan to prepare you for great responsibilities."**[50]
> **(Napoleon Hill)**

Failure makes success feel so much better. How can anyone truly appreciate blissfulness if they have never experienced despair? Imagine digging for a beautiful diamond for years, and you decide to quit just inches before you reach it? Would it be worse to live a life full of the pursuit of your passion rather than a "safe" life where you quit early due to fear and self-doubt? I prefer to die without those types of regret.

I appreciate the people that I have met over the past six or seven years. People have been really and truly encouraging in Belize, Mexico, Philadelphia, and even online. As someone without siblings or even a strong support system within my extended family, a lot of the advice and guidance that I received from these entrepreneurs and open-minded people have sustained me and kept me going. Someone I was close to had to remind me one day, like, "Don't compare yourself to anybody. You are rare." Again, this is not a message of exceptionalism. It is just a message of self-confidence – how not to externalize our confidence and try to be like anyone else – we can only be ourselves.

How that reminder reflected the space I must have been in where I felt inferior to someone else further along on their wellness journey. I get hard on myself a lot, as if I don't know that it's a marathon, as if I expect to have everything together overnight. Or even as if it's a lifestyle that I'll have altogether in a few months; this journey is a lifelong process, and my health goals are more based on longevity, feeling good, and being an active parent than trying to get a perfect body. Again, I was reminded not to compare myself to anyone else. Just simple as that. When I was going through some things, a sister simply told me, "Keep your head up." Words do matter.

I had a mentor tell me, "I see you working really hard, it seems like you're spinning your wheels, and it's time to start working smarter." In addition, these people understand what it is and what it takes to start your own business or build a brand from scratch. This is practical advice that I knew I could use. Not advice that says, "Stop what you are doing, return to work immediately, and build up someone else's empire," or "Stop building air castles," or rose-colored glasses, or any of the things many doubters say that destroy your confidence.

I appreciate those new people. These are the people that I eventually began to cultivate my circle of influence with. The people that have and are accomplishing the goals that I eventually aspire to. I remember one sister told me, "You don't owe anybody anything. You deserve to pick and choose whom you want to work with. Just because someone approaches you about an opportunity does not mean that you have to jump on it. You are not thirsty; you are valuable. You choose." That message really resonated with me. From that point on, I began to recalculate my workloads and really appreciate what I bring to the table, hone in on my skills, fine-tune the ones that needed tightening, and develop new skills that could benefit my overall business strategy.

Finally understanding that unless I knew my worth, I would constantly be trying to beg for $100 gigs. I would always be struggling. People would only give me what I asked for if they were even willing to give me that. However, the moment I knew my worth and carefully chose my clients, my service was on a request basis, by application, or invitation-only. Until I respected myself to that extent, I would always be a slave to my business and the demands of others. Own your time, own your life.

"In Japan, there is a term used to express the concept of 'constant and never-ending improvement,' Kaizen. The word Kaizen is actually a combination of two words: Kai, meaning change; and Zen, meaning good."[51] The idea is that improvements, no matter how small, will lead to great achievements. "It is a Japanese business philosophy regarding the processes that continuously improve operations and involve all employees. Kaizen sees improvement in productivity as a gradual and methodical process."[52] It is important to train ourselves to form beneficial habits through very small steps, as large-scale resolutions are usually difficult for most to maintain. Baby steps are key for anyone who wants to program themselves with new habits.

Self-efficacy & Emotional regulation. "Self-efficacy is a personal judgment of how well or poorly a person is able to cope with a given situation based on the skills they have and the circumstances they face.[53] Self-efficacy affects every area of human endeavor.[54]" It "refers to an individual's belief in his or her capacity to execute behaviors necessary to produce specific performance attainments (Bandura,1977,1986,1997). Self-efficacy reflects confidence in the ability to exert control over one's own motivation, behavior, and social environment."[55] Having total belief in yourself that you can competently take on the challenges at hand and the ability to navigate external criticisms and self-doubt with mastery. "'Emotion regulation' is a term generally used to describe a person's ability to effectively manage and respond to an emotional experience. People unconsciously use emotion regulation strategies to cope with difficult situations many times throughout each day."[56] Strengthening this skill will prevent us from allowing temporary internal emotions to have significant impacts on our permanent physical reality.

I've failed to learn to create a rhythm to my home life and maintain a balance with my work life. This may seem simple, but the levels necessary for homeostasis are always shifting when you lead a nomadic life. I've decided to make this stressor into a teacher. Constant change calls for greater adaptability. Adaptability is necessary to become sovereign in a rapidly evolving world. Things are changing faster each second: new policies, new industries, new challenges, and so much more. The only way to survive and thrive, these days, is to adapt.

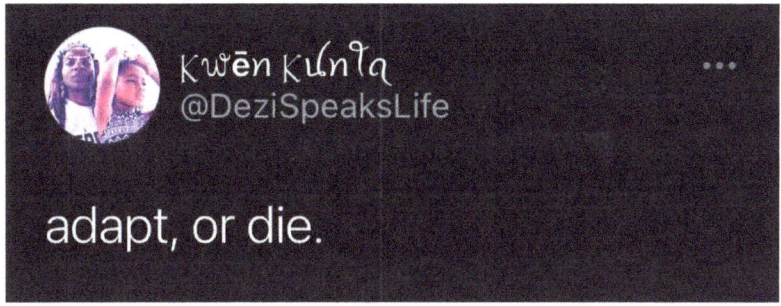

We All Lose Sometimes. This I will be 'realistic' about. I often say that I always call for the best while preparing for the worst. Like death, I don't see loss as an end. I know that things will bounce back better in due time. That belief is my safety net. Advance mental preparation virtually eliminates devastation by disappointment. This way, you are not naive to the flexural motion of life and seldom caught by surprise. I have not found that this practice has attracted more misfortune to my life overall, but I do feel like it has increased my resilience.

How fun could a game be if you won every round? Life needs texture and nuance. Try not to magnify your losses. Minimize them as lessons and necessary experience. They say Rome wasn't built in a day; the truth is, nothing great is thrown together quickly. One takeaway from this work should be quality over quantity. Progress is a time-consuming process requiring more depending on our level of dedication and natural aptitude. The fastest way to eat an elephant is one bite at a time – if that's the kind of thing you're into.

When we begin to rush ourselves, chances are we're falling into traps of comparison. Focus on your journey. You're the only one on your path, no matter how long it takes. When tuned into your own life, no one can possibly play your role; what's for you is yours alone.

Many times, to get on the right vibrations, we have to switch frequencies. We literally have to move ourselves mentally, spiritually, and maybe even physically to align with our visions. It's not possible to have the life you want by doing what you've always done or taking advice from people who have never made it happen. A removal of the chains of others' opinions and doubts of ourselves has to take place.

I had a discussion one day with an older Black gentleman, a kind fellow and former Chair of Finance in the Ohio House of Representatives. We were discussing my life and how I was a single mother, and he asked me about my son and showed interest in me as a person. As an intern then, most people just walked past me as if I was invisible. Therefore, it was nice to have someone with so much influence wanting to have a conversation with me about my life.

I told him about John, his age, and let him know how smart, talented and creative he was. He told me that he wanted me to make sure that my son was a master in three things by the time he graduated high school. He told me that he should be a master in a foreign language, a sport, and an art form. He even went as far as to say to me that if I enlisted him in these activities, he would pay for half of them. I was impressed, and I'm not so much a respecter of persons, but his compassion and consideration moved me that day. I totally appreciated the concept, and from that point on, I decided to focus not so much on collecting certifications or degrees but actually building life skills. It is the same for all of my children.

Some of these skills would include learning Spanish and especially how to sustain ourselves without being dependent on governmental systems. Another skill would be how to create our own food, farm, or garden, identify edible foods, and defend ourselves in physical conflicts. My son tried boxing, and now I am making sure that he is learning taekwondo. In addition, we did a lot of kickboxing in Belize. We are building tangible, real-life skills because as I think of the societies we have established over the past 100 years, we've really just begun to idolize careers that do little to benefit the people. I do not mean that in any offensive way.

For example, farmers do not get the respect they deserve considering that they are actually creating life-sustaining substances. They create food, and we need food in order to live. Scientists come up with innovations and creations that shape societies and civilizations. When there are food and water shortages, who is coming up with the solutions? The engineers are coming up with the mechanisms to desalinate the water or develop waste management systems. Who is coming up with these strategies that are keeping us alive, the things that matter? This is not intended to stress people who have dedicated themselves to careers that are now being automated. Much like a solid financial portfolio, our skill sets could be more diversified.

Nevertheless, I think that when it comes to what matters for the future, we should start focusing on innovating for sustainability and building skills that prepare us to innovate sustainably. We know that the planet is shifting, and we see the economy going in an electric and digital way. We see that certain careers will not exist anymore, and we may need to figure out how to survive the way people did generations ago. It has not been that long since we have been made absolute dependents for everything we need. In most US cities, residents would not know where to find drinkable water if they had to, let alone all the other necessities to live independent of external providers.

Chapter IX
RESILIENCE.

The Importance of Self-Determination and Skill-Building

I was eight months pregnant with my daughter Freedom when we returned to Belize in 2016. We were alerted that Hurricane Earl, a massive system, was on its way to Belize, and as we had moved up to the mountains of Cristo Rey, we wasted no time preparing for the hurricane by gathering pounds of rice, beans and drinking water jugs. We stashed buckets of water around the house for cleaning as it was customary for the water to go off quite easily. However, we had not experienced it to its full extent as yet. Hurricane Earl arrived, and it was crazy. The rain poured down in torrents, and the effects of the rain were immediate and tangible. Somebody up the mountain was having a baby, and an ambulance was trying to navigate the pouring rain and the stormy conditions to get to them. Houses and cars rushed down the river, and the main bridge to town was destroyed and was unusable for a few months.

We were actually concerned that there would be no bridge if I went into labor with my baby Freedom, and we had to go to the hospital. The power and the water were off for three days, and sometimes the temperature passed 100 degrees F. The people of Belize dealt with it so gracefully, as if everything was nearly normal. Everybody had already filled up whatever butane tanks they needed, people had their buckets of water for washing, they were cooking their rice and beans, and they already had their meat preserved. Some of the people in the village where we lived did not have running water and power previously so their shops, the roadside markets they had set up, were still operating. If this had happened where I came from, in the city, in the United States, it would have been pure chaos. People cannot seem to function without the basic necessities being provided for them conveniently. I am confident that it would have been sheer madness.

They would have had to call in for some additional military support to handle that type of situation in any major city in the United States. In Belize City, the people dealt with it well because they knew how to survive and manage their basic necessities. In addition, I think that we have developed a culture that looks down on that. Therefore, there are so many labor jobs that very few people are trained to take because at least two generations have looked down on those jobs in pursuit of degrees and other paper accolades. It is paper, so what can you do when it all comes down to it – when the lights go out? What can you create with it, but a larger fire?

Are you going to argue your way into some more water? What are you going to do, customer service yourself into some food? What can you do when your life is in danger? Can you defend yourself if no one is coming to save you? What can you do? Sovereignty means that you can take care of yourself, that you are responsible, and are able to respond. We should no longer applaud absolute dependence. If we are looking for freedom, we should know that freedom is not convenient. We romanticize freedom, but most people do not want freedom. Rich or poor, many people are entirely too dependent. They may want a more convenient life, or they might just want to feel better. Nevertheless, freedom takes work and creativity.

Freedom also takes resilience, self-determination, and skills. You have to be able to bring something to the table. What can you do that is actually necessary? Do you have the skills to be in the medical field? Can you teach, design, grow, sew, or build? What valuable set of knowledge can you pass into the future? What are you good for at the end of the day? What skills can you contribute in the real world? Not the plastic world, this synthetic polyester-blend illusion that is melting in front of our faces. Who have you developed yourself into?

I made it my life's goal to always keep learning. Not signaling that I've got it all figured out. However, I feel that at this point, I am all in on what I do know. Do you know what I mean? I'm here to write a book and share what I've gathered up until this point. I've been actively looking for lessons. Therefore, I can share with you what it is that I'm sure of. I'm undoubtedly certain that skills are necessary because, without skills, you are dispensable; you are actually unnecessary in a real world when all you have to bring to the table is your appetite.

If you have no skills, you become what some communities consider a "useless eater." What can you learn to do? No one wants to be useless. At the end of the day, we do not want to find out that we can do nothing when all the paper burns up. Then, we will have to be late starting to find out that we don't have any practical skills. We have to develop life skills, no matter your career, who you work for, or who you think you are – you have to learn how to do something. I do not care what organization you belong to or what position you hold within these systemic establishments – it does not matter; you need to develop life skills. Conflict resolution, emotional intelligence, and other character development techniques, the ability to work with and manage various human interactions, are also valued skills.

At the end of the day, you are a person on this planet, and when the falsehoods are stripped away, everyone is left with only what's in their minds and imaginations. What can be permanent are the mental treasures that are intentionally stored up. Some people craft themselves into who they want to be. They don't just surrender to the programs that we consume on the television and through our smartphones, what our bosses tell us to do, and who our pastors tell us we should be; but they do what they know to be true for themselves, and what is necessary.

Be the kind of person that you want to spend time with. Be the kind of person that you want around your children. Help shape them into the people that you want to raise your grandchildren, with intention, the kind of people to whom you want to entrust the future of humanity. Build your families and your tribe with intention. Develop skills, teach them skills, and identify their skills early while also shedding the arrogant parental control systems that try to make other people live out a path that is not theirs. Many parents try to duplicate themselves onto their children. What are their talents? What did they come here to do? Let's cultivate and invest that in our children. Do not make them live through what you lived through.

Please give them the best world possible with the best chances of succeeding in the lifestyles that they choose. That is evolution. We build skills and build the foundation, while they stand on that platform, and develop it. We pay it forward, and we pass it down. It does not have to be your child; it is the future. You are building the future. It could be someone else's child that you mentor. You may not have children, which is even more beautiful because you are just building for the future. It matters because apathy has gotten us to the point that we are at now, not caring. Too many of us are cognitively dissonant, not wanting to realize unfolding truths and open our eyes to a changing reality because regurgitating history has become so comfortable and convenient.

CHECK *Chapter X* YOURSELF.

Accepting Responsibility for Life Choices and Opportunities for Growth

"Accountability is when an individual … **experiences consequences for their performance or actions**. … Without it, it is difficult to get people to assume ownership of their own actions because they believe they will not face any consequences."[57] There is significant value and liberation in taking ownership of your decisions. Choosing to be the victor or the victim can only occur internally. I voluntarily took big chances that carried heavy consequences. Those consequences cost me the freedom I cherished so dearly, yet it was still my responsibility to carry that weight. No one made my ultimate decision but me. There are no saviors or quick fixes in real life.

Responsibility. How we choose to treat other people is very important. What I will share next is a major key to accountability. When we have been in situations where we felt truly powerless or oppressed, it can create a cycle where we replicate the treatment we received against someone else. Most times, this is difficult for us to recognize in ourselves, so I will offer an example. A father may be at work all day being treated poorly by his employer, and in order to maintain that employment, he swallows his feelings. When he arrives home, some of the same behaviors used against him may be passed on in the way he treats his wife. This is usually unintentional. In turn, she may feel that she has to hold her tongue out of appreciation for his sacrifices yet takes out her frustrations on their children. They may begin to treat each other poorly as a result. This is a written illustration of one type of cycle within the oppressed state of mind. In too many cases, the feelings are passed on to those most vulnerable in our care or who we perceive as beneath us in position. We should try to consciously treat others the way we want to be treated. None of us are perfect in this, and most still experience weaker moments. Yet it is still our duty to remain conscious of our behavior and how it affects those we say we love. If an employer treats you disrespectfully, the best solution is to quickly upgrade your skills and develop a certain exit strategy.

These cycles can be seen in the frustration levels of people who cannot find employment to sustain their families. They may frequently face trouble with authority figures when they leave their homes, and this can also be observed in young people who face constant bullying. The negativity can wear a person down and cause them to become fatigued in simply living their daily lives. Too many times, their consciousness is not developed to the point that they can prevent replicating the harm. Sometimes they harm themselves through coping mechanisms such as substance abuse, other addictions, and even suicide. Healing is especially necessary in these situations because these cycles can carry serious snowball effects generationally. Oppressed people must regain their humanity and knowledge of self in order to truly walk the course to liberation.

It's easy to feel discouraged when someone we depend on commits to doing something for us or assures us that everything will be okay, and the reality turns out differently. Many times, the people in our lives have good intentions for us, sometimes they don't. Our primary job is not to ponder on the intentions of others but to set our own. It's time to take full responsibility for the happenings in our lives – no more externalizing blame. Internalize Responsibility. In adulthood, no one owes us a thing. We do owe ourselves everything. I am not your guru; in fact, no one is. Self-healing brings true freedom.

One night in 2014, while I was still working at the asset management firm in Philly, I woke up at 4 am from a distressing dream. In the dream, I was scrolling through my timeline when I learned that my paternal grandmother had died alone at her kitchen table in Ohio. When I awoke, I immediately called my dad, who still lived in Ohio, and my uncle, who lived with her, and they confirmed she was alive. Later that day, I began my plans to relocate her to Philadelphia with me so that I could take care of her.

Most people I shared this plan with told me I had on "Rose-Colored Glasses," or something to that effect. I was thinking of leaving a job with bonuses, opportunities for advancement, employee shared ownership programs, and membership to professional organizations so I could stay home and be a caretaker for my grandmother, who had Alzheimer's. My uncle needed to be relocated as well, and then there was the larger issue of where they will live. Finally, it was decided that they would stay with my mother, who had recently retired and was in need of a situation that could supplement her finances, as well as a couple of my cousins who lived with her.

During that time, we were able to sustain over 12 people off the incomes of barely three. There were years of bad times, good times, and even more love, but it eventually got to the point that she could no longer function in the home. I had planned to take her to Belize so that we could try to heal her by using natural medicine, but my lovely grandmother died overmedicated in a nursing home anyway. I did not handle the aftermath of this situation gracefully, and I lashed out at others and externalized blame. For a few good hours, I became a virtual monster to people who had not made the decisions that I did. That was regretful. I checked my mirror, made my apologies, and things have continued peacefully.

Kwēn Kuntla
@DeziSpeaksLife

At some point we have to stop blaming others for the skills we lack, or unwanted habits we've developed environmentally. 'Cause while it might not be Our Fault, it SURE AS HELL is Our Problem. To #Fix.

Truth can be found in a rock, stream, online video, and even from an enemy. A late teacher once told me, "Don't throw the baby out with the bathwater." This stuck with me. Truth can be found anywhere. It becomes our duty to carefully dissect messages to filter the truth from the agenda. While this may seem tedious, anyone stepping into their personal power must understand that every moment in life holds a lesson. It is our job to learn the said lesson or continue to repeat the course. We need to take in the messages, listen critically, find the facts, and if it doesn't apply, let it fly!

"Accountability breeds response-ability."[58] (Stephen Covey)

Own Your Mistakes. It becomes easy to talk about the injustices we face when we believe we were treated unfairly or even bullied. I had a mentor who once reminded me, "You haven't always been so nice, either. Have you?" Rarely do we witness people discuss the wrongs they've committed against others, let alone honestly acknowledge their contribution to a disagreement. It will be hard even to find such stories online. Most people avoid accountability like the plague. If you truly want to get to know someone, ask about the times they've been cruel or when they have been the liar. Their sincerity in answering may matter more than the answers themselves.

There is true strength in vulnerability. If you are ashamed of who you are, why should anyone else trust you? Can you understand the strength that it takes to be vulnerable with anyone, especially the masses? Transparency is a signal of trustworthiness or integrity. I recognize that if someone is being honest with me, especially about their mistakes, it automatically gives me a higher level of respect for that person. I naturally don't respect labels, titles, or positions as much as I respect genuine integrity.

Time Management. We most admire people who are usually very effective time managers or closely associated with some. Not sure if it's an oversimplification, but I will say that the way we choose to manage our time and resources directly reflects our level of success. Sometimes, we think we don't have enough time to exercise, but we have enough time to watch the news. We believe a free online course is too time-consuming, but we can stream hours of an online series. We all have 168 hours in each week that we can organize into the most effective lifestyle possible. As a Study Skills Coordinator with the Bridge Program at OSU's Office of Diversity and Inclusion, it was part of my job to teach proper time management skills to incoming freshmen.

Over time these lessons, in addition to the various learning styles, have stuck with me the most. Since that time, I have learned that time is the most valuable asset we have during this life. We can correct things we have mismanaged, create long-standing institutions, develop ourselves into masters, and build bountiful, healthy nations with time. Time managed wisely can lead to the highest levels of abundance. Trading time for money is not equivalent because money can never naturally grant us more time. A wise investor can make money while she sleeps. Choosing to use our most vital years investing in our health, skills, and future will grant us more time to enjoy earthly freedom in the not-too-distant future.

The choices we make with our time gradually become our habits, and eventually, those habits develop into our character. It is surely a great thing that the character that we eventually shape is chiseled directly through our choices. Who we spend time with, the activities we engage in, and what we choose to consume. Your time is an asset spendable only by you. Use it wisely.

Deferred Gratification & Impulse Control. It's very important to make sacrifices that will take you further in life, such as cutting down on content streaming time, not eating junk foods, getting out of stagnant relationships, and other things that feel good or familiar but take us absolutely nowhere in life. Hanging with drifters will leave you drifting. Allowing yourself to be misused will keep you a victim. Constantly giving in to food and other addictions will destroy your body and shorten your lifespan. All of these issues will make us less than effective human beings, partners, and parents. They will distract us from our purpose and potentially even ruin the little time we do have left. By deciding to do what's most important now, we are promising ourselves a better future. Through the deferral of gratification or pleasure until the appropriate time, you will feel you have truly earned it, and what you desire post-transmutation will usually be of much higher quality. Who would want to ruin all of that hard work? Initially, it may feel like our impulses are working against us, and sometimes they are, as our brain seeks what's most familiar and convenient to get the satisfaction it craves. Over time we become the masters of our own destinies, and we will easily control those impulses. Though a cheat meal can enhance the quality of life through happiness, every so often, always aim for the good stuff. :)

"**Accountability is the glue that ties commitment to the result.**"[59] (**Bob Proctor**)

Be honest with yourself about your goals and the sacrifices you are willing to make to attain them. Do the work! Procrastination and fear delay not only yourself but your loved ones and your community that needs your abilities. Acknowledge your shortfalls and work to correct them. We can learn from anyone what to avoid and what to pursue. Be coachable when directed by a proper teacher. This will require the ability to accept honest criticism and guidance without the need for constant external validation from just anyone with an opinion. A true teacher has your best interests at heart. A hater secretly does not want you to be successful at the challenges they were too afraid to try or could not complete themselves. Remember, familiarity can easily breed contempt, unfortunately.

> **"Or how can you say to your brother, 'My brother, let me cast the chip out from your eye, when behold, the plank that is in your own eye is not visible to you? Hypocrite! First cast out the plank from your own eye, and then sight will be given to you to pull out the chip from your brother's eye." (Luke 6:42)** Aramaic Bible in Plain English[60]

Sometimes our glasses are crystal clear, but our mirror is still pretty dirty. Fix yourself before you try to fix others. A hurt person can only do more damage than a well person. That should be scripture. In a perfect world, self-healing would be a necessary prerequisite to leadership (including a family, team, or business). Be 100% transparent with yourself about what it is that you need to work on and do the deep and serious work on improving who you are as a human being. Only when you are hundred percent honest with yourself can you be truly honest with anyone else. If you are not honest with yourself, you can only project personal messages of self-contempt and inadequacy onto other people. This is why you find that the most miserable people are usually the loudest haters. If you constantly say negative stuff to other people and about other people, you may be a hater; please consider doing some deep introspection and personal work to fix yourself. Healthy-minded people live to uplift and encourage others to be the best versions of themselves. They celebrate and feel joy for the successes of others in their circle. They know their purpose on this planet is to contribute, not to energetically be a burden, but a blessing.

We currently exist on a plane(t) full of poisons & distractions at every turn, along with their cures and solutions. Healing is a lifelong process, and I believe few people ever to exist have been fully healed. With that, know that healing begins the moment that you decide to dedicate yourself to that endeavor; self-healing is inspiring to watch and can become contagious. You can be leading people unintentionally just through the decision to become your best self. It may be the hardest task you will ever undertake in life, but I would bet that it is by far the most rewarding.

Renew Your Spirit. Release negative thought patterns and just let that "baggage" go. Forgive yourself and cleanse through prayer, smudging, meditation, bathing, etc.; whatever your preferred (preferably harmless) ritual, use it! Launch a new beginning! When we begin to respect ourselves, we realize that our time, resources, and energy must also be respected. We understand our importance and no longer "cast our pearls before swine." Boundaries call for respect, and not everyone will like that. Not everyone is going to like you either, and that is perfectly fine. Respect doesn't require 'likes' and cannot be demanded, but rather commanded. Set boundaries for your relationships (interpersonal or professional), respect the boundaries of others and realize when any boundary (which limits you unnecessarily) must be adjusted.

Success Begins With Self-Respect. Of this I am also certain. Respect your value, time, being, and purpose while showing respect for your path and honoring your journey. "It means knowing what you stand for and what your values are, and being accepting of both your strengths and weaknesses. Self-respect is **an inner quality that each individual must take time to develop**. It comes after experiencing setbacks and failures throughout life and knowing how to rebuild."[61]

Respect Yourself / Being!

-   Respecting Your Body.
-   Respecting Your Space & Environment.
-   Respecting Your Mind, Soul, & Spirit.
-   Re-Internalizing Respect

In Mindset - Updated Edition: Changing The Way You Think To Fulfil Your Potential, Dr. Carol S. Dweck writes, "Believing that your qualities are carved in stone — *the fixed mindset* — creates an urgency to prove yourself over and over. If you have only a certain amount of intelligence, a certain personality, and a certain moral character — well, then you'd better prove that you have a healthy dose of them. It simply wouldn't do to look or feel deficient in these most basic characteristics… There's another mindset in which these traits are not simply a hand you're dealt and have to live with, always trying to convince yourself and others that you have a royal flush when you're secretly worried it's a pair of tens. In this mindset, the hand you're dealt is just the starting point for development. This *growth mindset* is based on the belief that your basic qualities are things you can cultivate through your efforts. Although people may differ in every which way — in their initial talents and aptitudes, interests, or temperaments — everyone can change and grow through application and experience." [62]

Discipline and Self-Control. We have to be honest with ourselves. How much work are we willing to do? How much time are we willing to sacrifice? After committing to a growth mindset, we must set in motion a plan of action to ensure the success of our goals. This will be only our responsibility to adhere to. If we don't develop discipline and self-control, we will always be under the control and discipline of something or someone else. Accountability partnerships are a great tool of support while building self-discipline.

Take Initiative. Create opportunities for yourself and others. Oftentimes, you'll be responsible for encouraging yourself and maintaining self-confidence. "Individuals who believe their talents can be developed (through hard work, good strategies, and input from others) have a growth mindset. They tend to achieve more than those with a more fixed mindset (those who believe their talents are innate gifts). This is because they worry less about looking smart and they put more energy into learning."[63] If anyone needs to keep convincing you to take charge of your own life, you are not yet ready.

Sometimes, we know our mindset is not where we want it to be at the moment, and we're just trying to hold it together for ourselves and our families. All we can do is hold our heads high and continue to do our best. We should remember to be gentle, as gentle with ourselves as we would be with someone else we care about during an instance of fragility. Do not allow anyone's opinion, including mine, to make you feel inadequate, as if you are behind or that there is something wrong with you. We have all been there, and sometimes I am still there. Sometimes, my words are not compassionate because I am not always the most merciful with myself.

A few people have called me a strict mother. I try to be structured with the older children as well as myself. I endeavor every day to shape myself into the person that I want to become. Some people close to me say that I push myself too hard, and I can feel when they're correct. There are consequences for that also. Sometimes, I am hard on my son, and I can recognize when that happens. I may see him working too hard on his schoolwork and getting an inferiority complex when compared to someone else, and sometimes, he cannot keep up with what I am requesting (or even demanding) at that time. Then I have to remind myself to be gentle; he is a great person, and he is growing into an amazing young man. These institutional education measurement scales should not be used to dictate his worth.

I should not allow him to feel inadequate if he doesn't always measure up to the world's standards because he already has. He was a member of the National Junior Honor Society. Things have not always been perfect, especially the last few years; we have all gone through crazy kinds of stuff. I remind him often that he is a much better person than I was at his age. In addition, I have to remind myself of that and not to be so hard on any of the children. They've also watched multiple loved ones die. Children will be children, but also do not be too hard on yourself. Humans will be humans. You know, it is not all about success. Maybe life is also not all about freedom and sovereignty. Maybe at the end of the day, the message should be about balance.

Perhaps it is all an illusion, and maybe peace of mind is the real goal. The peace of mind that comes through balance and having your basic needs met. I spent so much time desiring to be a billionaire and become successful, trying to live up to other people's expectations or prove them wrong, seeking to have it all and be able to fix the world's problems through ego-based ambitions. Now, I recognize that as I grow, all I need to do is be sustainable, happy, and surround myself with love to achieve true success; because love cannot be paid for no matter how rich a person is. Some things can never be purchased – love is one, and loyalty is another. You can pay somebody to be loyal if you want to, but let's see how loyal they really are when the money runs out. Same with love. You can pay someone to fake as if they love you. They will give you all the pleasure and attention you request, but when the money runs out, what will they give you then?

The real riches are in true love and peace of mind, not looking over your shoulder to see who is coming after your money bag, who is trying to hack into your account and take all the assets that you have hoarded. That is not the goal of life either. On this journey, I have realized that I want something new. My goals are shifting through the birth of this book, and I appreciate all of you for walking along this journey with me, witnessing the evolution of another human through their writing. I am not the same person as I was when I began writing this title, and I am eternally grateful for that.

It was not the goal to be, and I am not sure what the goal was. But maybe this is the reason that I had to complete this task. This was the assignment I gave myself; I wanted to write a book. I was not entirely sure what it would be about, and I had no idea how it would turn out, but I am grateful that it happened. Now there will be increased bandwidth available to focus on balance, peace of mind, and love. Please share.

As the founder of Young Black and Hustling, I have always resonated with the thought that you sleep when you die, no days off, grind time all the time. However, as I get older and experience more things and watch my children grow, I like to move my productivity more into phases and seasons. I feel that is only natural, much like the phases of the moon. There is a period when we experience a full moon, and then it wanes to a new moon and gradually waxes back into full. Everything in nature happens in phases. We have seasons: winter, spring, summer, and autumn, the rainy season and dry season, and the high season and the low season.

Even in the financial sector, there are multiple seasons; also, in food production, there are seasons. Therefore, I've decided to look at my life and levels of productivity from a seasonal standpoint. No longer am I going to go hard all the time, twenty-four seven and three hundred and sixty-five. Although, this may be because I put in adequate time to where I can actually begin to rest and reap the benefits of the many seeds planted over the past ten or fifteen years. At this point, for balance, I will commit to managing my productivity patterns on a seasonal basis.

For instance, as I wrapped up this piece, I began to think about the marketing plan, the music, the merchandise, and the tours. Yet mostly, I am looking forward to the period of rest that will follow; the work and focus on my family and health, the recuperation, and the rejuvenation. Yet every time I rest, and it is a suitable rest, I know that there is a period of intense "go-hardness" soon to follow.

I think this is a pattern that I will plan for the foreseeable future and the rest of my life. I no longer see the value in not resting and going hard twenty-four seven and grinding until I die. I feel like it was necessary to get my family and me to a certain point. I still believe that it may be necessary to help people overcome certain barriers, like the lack of determination or laziness, whatever you prefer to call it. However, once you get to a space where you are in the flow, producing, creating, and building your skills, there will then be time to rise, and, subsequently, time should be allowed for rest.

During the off-season, progress toward our goals doesn't die out – the movement never stops entirely. We simply grant ourselves an opportunity to slow down and refocus. Every cross-country road trip requires appropriately appointed times dedicated to personal and vehicular maintenance. Grab some good food, take a breather, hydrate, cleanse yourself, review the map, refuel the machine, and get great rest. Take the absolute best care of the mechanism that carries you through this life. That is the assignment.

Sometimes doing nothing is more important than doing everything. There are entire belief systems and religions surrounding the idea of doing nothing, of simply being – being a person who is enjoying the present – not always trying to graduate and hustle for a bigger future or the next big thing, but learning to appreciate and value what you have at that moment where you find yourself in the whole journey, and not just the destination. There is so much to value in the journey. That is one reason I like to overland versus flying. It is not so much about getting from point A to point B very quickly, but I love seeing the scenic topographical changes along the way.

At times you find yourself driving through the rain, and other times, you are driving through sunshine. You can go through a major location like Mexico City, while another time you are driving through the flat plains of Oklahoma. You might decide to camp in the Ozarks, chill out with llamas in Roswell, or make fried Oreos with friends in Chicago. You know, it is just about the journey, about enjoying every moment.

In 2015, when my family and I were driving cross-country down Route 66 and exploring so much of middle America, I really had a chance to appreciate what the United States of America has to offer outside of the impoverished city from which I came. The simple beauty of the spaces in between. There was so much nature left, undeveloped land in states like Alabama, and the people were so kind. There were so many small towns with hundreds of buildings that were just waiting for reinvestment, closed businesses, and dilapidated homes. Still, there was a talented and resilient population perfectly poised for new opportunities. There is so much beauty in the resting things and the commodities that do not seem to be glamorous.

Quality Time. There is tremendous value in simplicity – the minimalist life of just being, breathing, enjoying the sunlight, hydrating, loving and caring, cooking and cleaning, and spending time with your loved ones. There is so much joy to be found in that. Some people look at that as retirement, and I just look at it as a resting phase. Grind time comes, and when it comes, you go hard; you give it a hundred and ten percent with hardly any days off.

However, there also needs to be a natural phase where you know that you can anticipate rest. Just as a bear can enjoy and look forward to hibernation or birds can look forward to a time to migrate, it is only natural.

Humans seem to be the only creatures that push themselves to unnatural limits in the name of efficiency or acceptance. When we begin to align ourselves with nature, we realize that that capitalistic mentality that makes us max out and waste our limited youth on things that we cannot take with us is not sustainable. When we work through the need to collect riches and other physical things to impress people that we do not even like, we can authentically spend our life doing what we came here to do because we did not come to be slaves to money. None of us came here for that purpose. It is time to remember why we were born.

Chapter XI
FEAR LESS.

Letting go of fear-based baggage and being true to yourself.

"Fear is one of the **most basic human emotions**. It is programmed into the nervous system and works like an instinct. From the time we're infants, we are equipped with the survival instincts necessary to respond with fear when we sense danger or feel unsafe. Fear helps protect us."[64] Experiencing fear is totally natural; it's a part of what makes us human. All living beings have moments when they become afraid. However, to remain existing in a state of fear can paralyze us and make us continuously fearful – we will not be fearful people. "Fear of our own inadequacy drives us to scramble and scrounge, gasping for inspiration, but if we admit that the fear is a universal problem, we can get better at toughing out those dispirited moments and then decide more prudently what to do when we feel inadequate. Never stay in any situation that makes you feel inadequate."[65]

"Pure gold does not fear the smelter."[66] **~ Chinese Proverbs**

Life is not about finding yourself; it is about creating yourself. I will say this again – we are the masters of our own destiny. We shape the person that we become through our intentions and our actions. We directly affect our future and the futures of those closest to us. It is not someone else that will come, intervene, and build us into the person we are meant to be. They can mold you into the person they want you to be for their agenda, but no one can develop you into the person that you were created to be. You were predestined for your purpose.

Even our innermost desires are predestined; genetically, spiritually, and cosmically. You chose your purpose, whether you consciously remember it or not. It is something that we actively create and by actively, I mean it takes action – deliberate and conscious action. It takes **effort**. Greatness is not free If it were free, everybody would be great, and the Lord knows that not everybody is great. As much as we would like that to be the case, most people do not have what it takes to be great because they lack the self-discipline and determination to make it so. Given that all of these things are determined by our choices, we choose to actively create ourselves into the person we want to be. If we can visualize who we want to be when we die or at the height of our legacy, we need to make decisions that align us with the roadmap that can get us there. Any decision that we come across or make that takes us off that path is detrimental to the person we want to be. When we have a clear vision of what we want for our future, with praxis (when our actions and our mind start to align with our beliefs)3 we put ourselves into direct alignment in a quantum flow. It is not any religious "hocus pocus" but actual science; it's quantum physics.

When you do that, you are putting yourself into physical alignment on the vibrational frequency of the goal that you have strung and attached yourself to out there. It's coming, with time, depending on the scale of your vision. However, every decision must be carefully aligned with the person we want to be, consistent with the vision we want to create for the world we want to build.

Optimism. When we know we are doing the right thing, we can be confident that situations will eventually work in our favor. Every day, I am grateful for divine protection and guidance. The idea is to remain connected, develop faith in yourself and eliminate the shackles of fear. As a traveler, you have to release fear and accept that you are entering the unknown at some point. You're fully aware that you'll be discovering new things and will cultivate personal growth when processed with a proper attitude, shedding yourself of contracts that only maintain contact and leases that serve as leashes. We can begin to consider a life where our resources are not only working to maintain a life that we hate. The power is ours to decide how we will reallocate our funds and establish income replacement to bring us a life that includes bliss.

Everyone on this earth deserves joy; most perceived evil derives from stolen joy – an early sense of powerlessness and pain and a partial giving up on humanity and goodness in others. Hurt people literally hurt people. Releasing that hurt and pain can lead us to a life of freedom and the bliss we deserve. We all have made mistakes and will continue to make them. You are not "bad," you've been hurt. We can decide never to hurt anyone else again. We can decide to be the force that stops those cycles, the hero of our own story. Life is our hero's journey. Eventually, we all will grasp these concepts in one lifetime or another.

We were not created to be afraid of actually living. Fear prevents us from living the life we desire. Not necessarily fear of the dark (though in many ways it is), but also fear from the judgment of others. Don't be afraid of looking bad. Allow your journey to be authentic and your progress measurable. We can have all these preconceived ideas about what "they" will say. The "theys" that are smarter, wiser, holier, more ambitious, and prettier than us, even the "theys" that we already know don't like us. We foolishly live out our lives based on what we think they will think.

This is solely a personal problem, and many times they are focused on their own lives. The only thing you've accomplished is limiting yourself. Regardless, people will talk about you or someone else. If you're living big enough, more of "them" will notice when major changes are taking place. If they care about you, it may shake them up for a moment, but that moment will surely pass. As humans are known to do, they will adapt to the new situation, and everyone will find their fit (or not).

Mastery takes time and experience. This may vary depending on natural aptitude and access to supportive resources. However, mastery to any degree will require practice. It may not be your goal to become perfect, but as your mind and body adjust to new habits, the updates and improvements will become automatic. "In essence, Mastery is that **mysterious process during which what is a first difficult becomes progressively easier and more pleasurable through practice**. We describe it informally by saying that we can practice a movement until that point when we 'program it into the autopilot.'[67]"

Undefeated. The only people I'm trying to impress are my descendants and my ancestors. When we're tapped into this game called life, it becomes hard to recall why we came here. This matrix of illusions can get so distracting that we begin unconsciously playing with the jersey we're given. Imagine if every person was truly born free, fully aware of their sovereignty and ability to create their own lives. How much power would escape the "high" places?

What would it look like if we would stand firm in our sentience and not surrender our futures into the hands of others?

I was able to meet some of the most talented people in my life while I was in jail. I met people who could take Honey Buns, sandwich cookies, and other seemingly random snack items and sculpt beautiful birthday cakes, and tattoo artists who would translate their skills into drawing life-like caricatures of other inmates and guards. I had a friend named Fingerz or Dedos (in Spanish) who would keep us looking clean by threading our brows from the string pulled from Department of Corrections issued jackets. Talent can be found anywhere, but amazing talent does not complete the formula for success. Far too often, we let self-doubt, fear of failure, lack of tangible examples, and even negative opinions of others prevent us from living our best lives. I want everyone to feel empowered to own their strengths, develop strength around their weaknesses, and fearlessly push forward toward their life passions.

Self-Determination. "In psychology, self-determination is an important concept that refers to each person's ability to make choices and manage their own life. This ability plays an important role in psychological health and well-being. Self-determination allows people to feel that they have control over their choices and lives.[68]" I am always betting on myself 100% because I know I will never quit. Things will always get hard just as they always eventually get better. Who can you bet on to always do the best job they possibly can? Make that your core team and make sure that you are a good example. Sometimes it takes a while to identify that core team but always do your best even if you find yourself alone.

Kwēn Kúnta
@DeziSpeaksLife

Self-control is a most valuable asset..

Nothing short of death can stop the movement of my mind power. Develop yourself into an unstoppable force. Once you begin to cultivate your own thoughts, this would not only be a possibility but a probability. While I was writing this volume, my computer stopped working. There could have been excuses not to get it done, but there were none. I chose to continue this journey of reflection through a smartphone because the show must go on. Self-respect dictates that we're faithful to the promises we make to ourselves. If we can take a job and make someone else our superior, be on time for them, and comply with all of their requirements, then we should honor our personal commitments in the same way. This is the level of thinking that leads to freedom. Talent will only take a person so far. You can usually measure a self-made success by their level of mental resilience. Everyone will not get back up and cannot work well under pressure; everyone cannot handle criticism. Everyone can't even stick to their own schedules. Not everyone is going to become free. Consistency, frequency, and the absolute refusal to quit are what separates those who are not victims of fear.

"The elegance under pressure is the result of fearlessness.[69]**"**
(Ashish Patel)

I like to think of this as "flinchlessness." Yes, I just made that up the word "flinch-less-ness." It means that you might as well not even flinch in the face of fear. You've been through enough to know that whatever happens, everything will be alright. Even in death, everything will be alright. Tackle your challenges, and do not avoid them. There is no reason to hide who you are. Face life, and don't flinch. Fam, I tested myself on this one; since I made up the word, it was my responsibility to make sure it worked. So I decided to get a quick Brazilian wax at Bella Nail Studio across the street from our flat in Colosio. Ladies, some of you know the pain of this service, especially when it's been some time. Needless to say, I did flinch a lot! As a mother of three, I actually should have known better. While flinching might not always be controllable, I will say with certainty that you should not cower from painful situations. Life's not about playing Tough Tony, but it required some level of significant labor to get each of us here today. Astonishing goals are to be achieved on the other side of great discomfort.

Who remembers their childhood heroes? Those people who, in our eyes, could do no wrong? Now, back to reality! We are the heroes of our own stories, the authors of our own tales, and the painters of our own tapestries. Long gone are the times of externalizing our confidence in other mortal beings. You are the master of your own destiny. When we externalize our faith, we diminish what is left for ourselves. We become slaves to other people's approval and are willingly surrendering our personal sovereignty. When you are prepared to step into your power, your confidence is yours, for keeps.

Confidence is Key! Do you trust in yourself? Do you know that you're good enough? "Confidence is a belief in oneself, the conviction that one has the ability to meet life's challenges and to succeed—and the willingness to act accordingly.[70]" Aside from your mama or significant other, who will have confidence in you if you don't? Self-confidence is the only difference between mastery and slavery. When I got out of jail, I was totally depleted of confidence. Then I discovered "My Strong Reason Why" (to succeed). "Projecting confidence helps people gain credibility, make a strong first impression, deal with pressure, and tackle personal and professional challenges. It's also an attractive trait, as confidence helps put others at ease.[70]" Through building a solid network and practicing my confidence, I earned a better job than I ever had before.

What Other People Think Is Not Your Problem. Their thoughts about you are as frivolous as farts in the wind. If they think you're weird, they may just be super-ordinary. Unless they're paying for it (or you're hurting someone or thing), what you do is not their problem. It's not your responsibility to solve the problem that they have in their mind about you. The moment you start trying, you've become a slave to the opinions of others. Soon, you'll realize that your entire life is only a composite of what other people told you that you should do. If you become a failure, they will not take credit for that.

Rise Above the Haters. They are low vibrational beings. Some people think that your failure will prop them up, and it may do so temporarily. What they fail to realize is that their hating ways exhibit their personal misery. People stuck at the hater stage can't truly prosper. Some will enjoy reminding you of how you used to be. Many times, talking down on others makes miserable people feel better about themselves. You are not the person you were yesterday unless you choose to be. We have to rise above the opinions of others. Let them talk. Don't get mad. Allow it to fuel your motivation!

> ....they have to talk about you. Because when they talk about themselves, nobody listens.

I know it's not very positive, but I want to stick with this topic a little longer. People can't believe in you when they don't believe in themselves. When they're stuck with a lack mentality and unable to reach heart-mind coherence, they see someone who resembles them, and it reminds them of their own self-directed inadequacies. While we can blame others for our programming, we are responsible for the reprogramming. They might even hold higher esteem for people who least resemble them. This is because their concept of superiority has been fully externalized. Like a computer, they are running on an internalized inferiority complex operating system. Due to this fact, their hardware literally cannot process a program that sees someone like them ascend to great heights and actually appreciate it. These people remind them of their background, where they came from, and the many things they're most ashamed of. They often say, "How could this person achieve that? I never could." It's a constant comparison – a nearly inescapable loop of competing with people who don't even have them in mind. The evolution from that extremely low-level frequency is very difficult and nearly impossible. It would require some type of great awakening moment that becomes a total shift in consciousness. Also, self-awareness and discovery, and a sense of pride, not hyper-criticism, when watching familiar faces ascend. Yet those types of moments are usually self-led, and the type we're discussing tends to shy away from introspection. The special ones who seek and find that healing are beautiful souls who had just gotten injured along the way; misery was only a pit-stop.

Many of us have been there before, at a low point where it is hard not to view ourselves compared to others. Social media dictates that we view our lifestyles in parallel with what we scroll past. We are operating outside of purpose in these moments by not focusing on doing our very best in our own roles. Keep making progress and being proud of yourself. Celebrate yourself, and soon you will find no issue in celebrating others.

Set the tone for your relationships by the way you conduct yourself; people will know how they should approach you. The boundaries you set, early on, should be the boundaries you keep until someone has been properly vetted for acceptance into one of your inner circles. Swine don't deserve your pearls, family. With humility and grace, your presence can command respect without demands. If we allow anyone else to drain us for our energy on-demand, then we are their willing battery. Low vibrational beings cannot even connect to the frequency when we raise our own vibrations through self-love.

Fertile Ground. Ideas grow through you, and whatever you touch will flourish. You resonate with the frequency of life-sustaining sources, now a conduit for your Creator, to be used according to Its purpose. Nature herself will conspire to make sure your navigations are accurate and your works unfold as you are now connected to her eternal vibrations.

There was a stone in the ground, and the stone felt so alone. It knew of neighboring stones that would be plucked from the dirt and used in the most beautiful ways. The stone wondered why it was never taken from the ground and used in a beautiful way. She waited and waited and eventually forgot that it was alone, and that it was even a stone. Finally, centuries later, when it was plucked from the ground, its discoverer realized that it now had one of the most magnificent gems his people would ever see. The stone would now be used to create a beautiful thing.

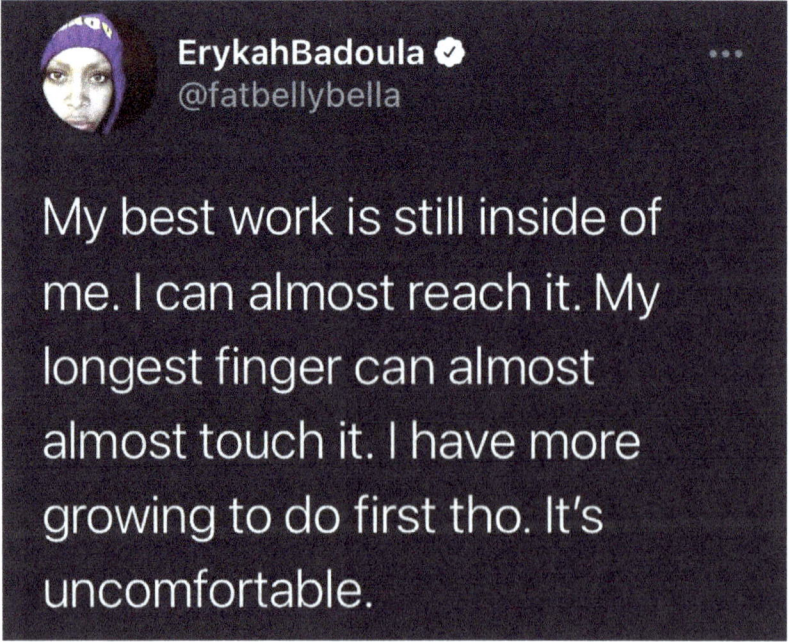

ErykahBadoula ✔
@fatbellybella

My best work is still inside of me. I can almost reach it. My longest finger can almost almost touch it. I have more growing to do first tho. It's uncomfortable.

Chapter XII
HUSTLING.

To be Aggressive, Especially in Business or Other Financial Dealings[71]

*E*xploring Entrepreneurship. Even if you're working for someone else right now, you should consider the long-term goal of business ownership. Try focusing some time on a product to develop, a service to offer, or a trade you could be passionate about. Your business could be an adult daycare, an online course, a recording studio, a photography company, childcare, tutoring, a farm, or maybe even a YouTube channel. Striving to provide the best for your loved ones doesn't make you money hungry. We should all be actively building this world together. Entrepreneurship does not mean you need to be tied to a brick-and-mortar building, in this new world. You could be an online investor, writer, content developer, create NFTs (Non-Fungible Tokens), a tradesperson in Information Technology (IT), or even build new worlds in metaverses – the lanes are now unlimited, it seems. As long as you're willing to monetize your skills, you can eventually achieve financial independence.

"Entrepreneurship is a personal growth engine disguised as a business pursuit[72]," tweeted James Clear. That resonates with truth; self-development disguised as business. Most people progress more through difficult times than they do in times of leisure. I can definitely say that rings true for me. Throughout my entrepreneurial journey and brands I have built, I have grown so much as a creator, mother, partner, daughter, and friend.

Entrepreneurship is not for the faint of heart. Entrepreneurship requires you to think for yourself and try to operate in the best interests of your team and your future. It requires you to be able to keep going no matter how many "nos" you receive, to face rejection, and not give up anyway. It's okay to take a break, but it's not okay to give up. It is okay to restructure your plans and rebrand yourself, reshape your identity, and continue to grow into the person you want to be at the end of the day.

Entrepreneurship, at its root, requires you to be firmly grounded in your purpose, in your mission, and get it done no matter what the cost because a real entrepreneur does not give up during the marathon. They may get a job that helps them finance their goals and to help them pay their bills so they can sustain themselves enough to continue working towards their vision.

Entrepreneurs don't quit. A true entrepreneur never retires. There is no magic age where an entrepreneur will say, "I think I'm going to stop visualizing." Entrepreneurs are visionaries; it is in their blood. We are not pleased with ourselves when we do not build something, think of something, or create something. A true entrepreneur is not just in it for the money. It is a lifelong process of building businesses, brands, legacies, and self. An entrepreneur never quits.

Entrepreneurial spirits are also contagious. Children raised by entreprenurs usually do not find joy in using all of their vital life force energy to fuel someone else's vision, especially when we discover and develop their uniqueness. They have seen the freedom that comes with setting your own schedule and spending your own time. In addition, the progress that comes with self-discipline and the ability to manage your own time and control your own life is very important to an entrepreneur.

"Keep cool when other people get hot.[73] **(Napoleon Hill)**

Entrepreneurs learn habits from their parents, like self-control and self-discipline. If you cannot discipline yourself, someone else will gladly do it for you. If you lack control over yourself, systems have been put in place to tackle that problem. Why should you not have power over your temper? Regulate your own emotions, and do not hand over your power button. Whether it is an individual, government, or institution, somebody will control your life. It might as well be you.

Entrepreneurship is the key to freedom. Investors are entrepreneurs; they allow their money to work for them. It is just another level, and there are many levels of business. Sometimes people look at entrepreneurship as a dirty word – people who do not work or people who do not want to get a job. That whole mindset is a program of its own. Many people don't realize that it's way more difficult to be an entrepreneur, make a schedule, stick to it, and develop the fortitude and resilience to continue working in the face of continuous rejection, to keep on trying and failing until you eventually succeed. That takes a unique spirit and a different kind of mind. It requires undying devotion to your purpose.

It's not the body that builds the business, it's the mental attitude. With the right idea, someone could use websites like Fiverr or Creative Fabrica, and build a multimillion dollar business without ever leaving the comforts of their home. A person, while still mentally weak, will never become a successful entrepreneur. A weak person may more likely get a job where they're told what to do and when. A mentally weak person can never build a successful brand from scratch, but they could possibly be hired to manage other people's affairs for them. They might show up for someone else, on that person's time, and gladly punch a clock during the hours provided for them and then do what they are told. It is not an inconvenience for them because it is easy to follow instructions, have your entire life structured for you, depend on someone else for your schedule, compensation, benefits, and to feed your family. It is not that complicated.

Everyone is not willing to take on the risks associated with becoming a lifelong entrepreneur – the serious risks of possibly not always having a roof over your head, sometimes sleeping in your car, having to eat imperishable foods because you cannot afford fresh groceries or prepare meals because you are reinvesting in your business. You take the risks because you're absolutely certain that long-term dedication and sacrifice are going to pay off.

Honestly, investing became a full-time goal for me because I despised the stress of working for someone else. Even when I worked outside of "Corporate America" as a contractor, I found myself putting too much energy into projects that had nothing to do with my vision and that I did not enjoy. Many times, I felt like the demand on my time and energy was not worth the compensation I was receiving, if I was even being compensated. At one point, I decided that I would let my employers know exactly what I wanted to be paid and began respecting my time with no apologies. Sometimes we had to part ways, and I was usually relieved.

"Don't spend major time on minor things"[74] **(Jim Rohn)**

The results should at least match the effort. I'm not going to beg anyone to support my business because it becomes exhausting. Time cannot be wasted trying to convince people to do things; therefore, the results have to speak for themselves. If it's great enough, they will be drawn; **if you build it, they will come.** Ultimately, I decided that my time was no longer worth trading for the tool of money. I would rather be cash broke for a season than in bondage for a lifetime. I knew that I had to find a way to make the money work for itself so that I could spend my time fulfilling my visions and caring for my loved ones. Cryptocurrency jumped on the scene like Superwoman herself, and I had discovered, at least, an initial step.

Have a Good Time. This one cannot be overstated. Loosen up. We came to this world to experience. God is experiencing life through our eyeballs. We speak directly to the Most High when we communicate with Its creations. In everything and in every place, It keeps everything moving. Life will always get harder, just as it always gets better. We do not have forever here, so I think we should put our time, which is our most scarce resource, to its best use.

FREEDOM.

Remember the Past. Act in the Present.
Do it for the Future.

"Freedom is no fairy gift to fall into a man's lap. What is freedom?
To have the will to be responsible for one's self." (Max Stirner)[75]

Free·dom[1] [76]
/ˈfrēdəm/
noun: freedom

1. **the power or right to act, speak, or think as one wants without hindrance or restraint.**
   "we do have some freedom of choice"

2. **absence of subjection to foreign domination or despotic government.**
   "he was a champion of Irish freedom"
   Opposite: dependence

3. **the state of not being imprisoned or enslaved.**
   "the shark thrashed its way to freedom"
   Opposite: captivity

4. **the state of being physically unrestricted and able to move easily.**
    "the shorts have a side split for freedom of movement"

5. **the state of not being subject to or affected by (a particular undesirable thing).**
    noun: freedom from; plural noun: freedoms from
    "government policies to achieve freedom from want"
    Opposite: liability

6. **unrestricted use of something.**
    "the dog is happy having the freedom of the house when we are out"
    Opposite: restriction

7. **familiarity or openness in speech or behavior.**
    plural noun: freedoms[2]

To remain dependent is the opposite of being free, whether it is on another person or a system. There are many levels of freedom in various categories, and this includes physical freedom, mental freedom, spiritual freedom, financial freedom, food security, and more.

Your Life is Happening Right Now. After a couple of months and spending a fair amount of money on my skilled legal team, I accepted a plea deal that would send me home from the county jail. The Class X was reduced to a Class 1, and I was released from Cook County Jail with two years' probation and a felony for the possession, manufacturing, and delivery of cannabis.

When I got out of jail, one of the first things I did was start a business called Oya Hair & Health in Philadelphia, PA; I called myself the Hair Weave Dealer. While this was profitable and allowed me to make some extra money, I did not feel any love or passion for the hair sales business and decided to re-brand the company much later. To this day, one of my most purposeful projects is Young, Black, and Hustling, LLC Social Network for Black-owned brands, bands, and businesses around the world. We hosted pop-up malls, parties, food giveaways, artist showcases, and other community events that received much love and support. This organization flourished, locally & online, until our first relocation to Belize in 2015.

Today I'm blessed to be able to wake up with my children, engage in physical activity, have breakfast, and plan out my day the way I want to. I have a teenager and two toddlers now, and as I write this, I am five months pregnant with a child who will likely be born in Mexico. My partner and co-creator of over eight years is tremendously dedicated and supportive. I know that this is a blessing, and every day I feel so lucky, even a healthy dose of survivor's remorse. By applying the right principles and thoroughly executing your passion, I know that you can also do this and so much more. Abundance is something I believe everyone deserves to experience. If you are working toward your goals consistently, you deserve to flourish, especially when what you're doing makes a positive difference to the world.

Your presence speaks to the fact that you are ascending to new heights in your mental and spiritual journey. We now live in a global society where social media keeps us fully immersed in the lives of others on a continual basis. It becomes hard not to consume the images presented and view them in contrast to our own realities. When we begin to find ourselves focused more on creating the lives we desire, we have little to no time left for critiquing (or comparing ourselves to) others, and happiness and fulfillment can only be discovered within. The process of uncovering our power is the journey to success. Just as the redwood seed inherently contains all of the genetic data required to become the largest living thing on earth, so do we. We are all mighty seeds, and digging deep within ourselves is the only way to strike the living waters necessary for germination.

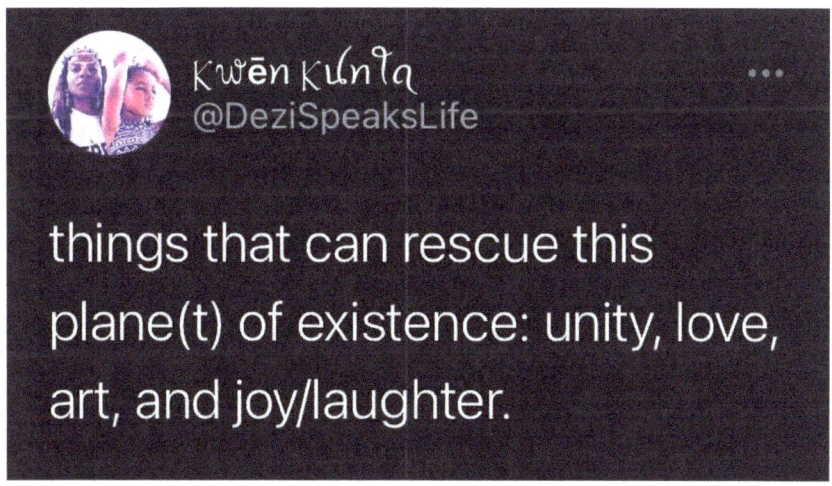

We Take Control of Our Realities. No one is coming to save us; our lives are our responsibility. No one can walk our paths for us, even if they wanted to. Our Salvation is in our hands. Free yourself from wondering if other people will like it. Free yourself from worrying about who will feel offended and from hoping that the multitudes show up. Free yourself from egotism and from thinking anyone is better than you. Free yourself from thinking you can't do it and that you don't deserve it. Free yourself from wishing you were somehow better than you are right now. Recognize that you are perfect and already house everything you need to become the greatest version of yourself. No one could ever be better than the greatest version of yourself, and at your greatest, you are not better than another. Once you decide this, it is already done.

A good elder once told me that our generation has a preoccupation with "consciousness" and being woke. That we should focus more and pick up more of a "responsibility consciousness." Some words can sting, but those stuck. We should seriously consider focusing our attention on the things that will benefit our children while teaching and showing them responsibly to do similarly for their descendants.

We need to get our hands dirty, boots on the ground, visualize our goals, and do the work. The work we do on ourselves may be the hardest work we ever undertake while letting go of outworn patterns, relationships, and circumstances.

If it is not working for you, helping to develop you to your highest self, or contributing to young overall well-being, then it's time to let it go. This may be the most difficult step for anyone beginning to own their personal power. It requires the breaking of hindering habits, parasitic partnerships, purposeless plans, and the lot. We must know our worth and innerstand that sometimes we have already given situations everything that we can. Basically, if it's not feeding you, it's consuming you. Sometimes they may still be expecting more because a precedent of continuous giving is what we have established. Other times we can become deeply involved in psychological co-dependence, causing its destruction to hurt us as well as anyone else involved. When we start loving ourselves more, we internally increase the value of our contributions and stop selling ourselves cheaply. We begin to invest ourselves responsibly. Not everyone can honor, accept, and appreciate this. That is why, in many cases, stepping into your power requires you to LET THOSE BAGS GO! It feels so good to walk freely.

Space and Breathing Room. I didn't realize, until recently, that I was making time for everyone else but myself. By the end of the day, I would be exhausted without having done anything relaxing for myself but sleep. I know this sounds like a norm for many of you, but I do not believe that life was intended to be this way. Constant stress, running around, jumping through hoops are some of the easiest ways to shorten your lifespan. Quite literally, stress can kill and act as food for cancer. The primary factor is the way we mentally process stress. Most of us process mental stress into physical anxiety. This anxiety impacts all of our bodily functions, including our breathing patterns. Some of us forget to breathe entirely, I've been there, and it still happens at times.

While I was doing taekwondo this morning, I realized that I still hold my breath when facing a difficult situation. It is almost like a trauma response, a bracing effect where I tend to hold my breath until a difficult moment has passed as if somehow, that makes things not feel as bad. Actually, not breathing tends to make things more difficult. As soon as I begin to breathe deeply through my nose and out through my mouth, every move that I execute becomes more fluid, the force behind it gets stronger. "Oxygen is used by all cells to convert food to useful energy. Proper growth of the fetus and placenta depends on the ability of the cells to sense oxygen. [77]" "Momentary stress causes the body to tense and you begin to breathe a little more shallowly. A shallow breath lowers oxygen levels in the blood, which the brain senses as stress. Breathing then becomes a little faster and shallower. Oxygen levels fall a little more[78]." Oxygen feeds the brain; "despite comprising only 2 percent of the body, our brains consume 20 percent of the body's oxygen supply[79]."

We Nourish Ourselves. Water, earth, fire, and air – this is what we are made of. Breathing is such an essential bodily function; no wonder it's involuntary. It directly connects to the circulation of our blood and the beating of our hearts. "The right side of your heart receives oxygen-poor blood from your veins and pumps it to your lungs, where it picks up oxygen and gets rid of carbon dioxide. The left side of your heart receives oxygen-rich blood from your lungs and pumps it through your arteries to the rest of your body".[80] Faster breathing fuels the heart, and it causes heat to increase throughout the body. Water is shed to cool the body, and slower, deeper, and more conscious breathing calms the heart. This calmness spreads through other body systems, our resting heart rate optimizes, and we enjoy increased mental clarity and awareness. We are able to adapt to various stressors much more fluidly. This adaptation, and newly found ease in decision-making, makes life going forward much less stressful. We automatically begin making healthier decisions that increase our longevity. Breathing is life. We breathe and release stagnant energy.

It is so pertinent that we innerstand how our environment, lifestyle choices, clean nourishment, and daily habits reflect our health and longevity. It will also reflect the same for all of those in our care or under our leadership. Health is wealth, and healthy choices signal responsible thinking.

The moment I hit the road, I appreciate the openness and space that being outdoors provides. My constant desire to travel could be a manifestation of my desire to escape the current reality. Without awareness, this has become easily the most beneficial way to cope with my emotions. Alternatively, with awareness, I can curate a lifestyle from which I need no escape. Through the non-profit MasterMind Cooperative, our team will be offering family-friendly experiences at various international permaculture campuses. Each experience will be facilitated by a carefully selected and highly competent team member, focusing on recreational health.

Through a fellowship with Fit to Navigate (a program that seeks to combat recidivism, with a particular interest in mothers) in 2019, I became a certified Fitness Trainer, later deciding to rebrand Oya Hair & Health into The Well-Being Specialist and Growing Young Apothecary. We focus on helping people strategize healthier lifestyles while focusing on longevity and anti-aging. This information is to be studied, passed down, and built upon generationally. Services will be provided at our international permaculture & wellness campuses in partnership with The MasterMind Cooperative. This project is currently under development in Quintana Roo, Mexico, and the Cayo District of Belize.

> **"There can be no real freedom without the freedom to fail."**
> **(Eric Hoffer)**[81]

Blessings in Adversity. There are significant advantages in being disadvantaged and major disadvantages in being advantaged. I recently read an article that listed three benefits of struggle. One was that it gives you empathy; secondly, it teaches where you need the most improvement, and lastly, it builds character. "The grind can be a cruel teacher.[82]" Without the freedom to fail, resilience cannot be built. Resilience develops when you feel the fire under your bottom without a safety net. Freedom requires resilience because freedom is not always comfortable; in fact, freedom is not for comfort. Freedom is for sovereignty and to be able to live your life on your terms. It is not about depending on someone else for your food, income, or personal security. To be clear, freedom does not mean success to everyone.

> **"Where there is no vision, the people perish..." (Proverbs 29:18)**[83]
> King James Version

Vision and Visibility. Creating a clear vision of the life you want to lead is the first step to making it a reality. You want the vision to become so clear that you can even smell, hear, and feel it. The feelings of fulfilling this goal will become as real as what you ate this morning. Using the principles described earlier in this book, your vision will begin to materialize sooner or later, depending on its size and scale. I share this because I know it to be true, from personal experience. We are now preparing to move into the most spacious home I've ever lived in, surrounded by nature, rooms, and bathrooms for everyone, and all by "coincidence," but I don't believe in coincidence. Building good karma keeps me in a state of "pronoia." The real blessing is that just by anticipating the idea of living in this home, the peace of mind granted has helped ease writer's block. Breathing room, wooooosah.

With no hope and without vision, it's no wonder the people perish. It's not hard to cut something short when it's going nowhere and you're suffering. What's the purpose of cherishing life? What is the purpose of life? Shaping a vision can save a community or even a world. The size of the vision, and the further it is from your current reality, will certainly impact the amount of time it takes to materialize, but through intentional consistency and directed intensity, the vibrational frequency is constantly attracting our corresponding outcomes.

Other people might not understand your vision, especially at first, and that is totally okay. What's given to you is for you. Sometimes we have to make things tangible for people in order for them to truly believe it's possible; even then, there will be deniers. That is not the focus; stay true to your mission and those who help make it a reality.

> **"The human mind treats a new idea the same way the body treats a strange protein; it rejects it." (Peter Medawar)**[84]

Being a role model to people from a familiar background can be a powerful position. You are able to inspire and uplift others who can relate to you. You can help them believe that accomplishing their goals is possible. Share your story and walk in your truth; the world could always use more good examples.

"Vision Without Action is a Daydream, Action Without Vision is a Nightmare" [3] - quote taken from the blog "Where there is no vision, the people perish[85]" by Aidan McCullen

---

Your vision will be so clear that the steps to its actualization will fall easily into place, sometimes, seemingly without any further effort than clarifying and building beneficial karma toward your vision. You will be able to recognize them almost immediately, and it will become easier with time. This is the place where the karma we discussed earlier becomes most important. If you have no goals and dreams, you might be free to create whatever kind of karma falls in your way. However, if you know you are going to create a legacy of greatness, you are extremely intentional about the karma you shape for yourself and your loved ones. In everything, there should be applied intention. Your steps should be ordered toward action that furthers your mission. Directed action fuels the mission. The energy you intentionally surround yourself with will dictate the efficacy of your actions.

"If you can hold it in your head, you can hold it in your hand." [86]
(Bob Proctor)

They say that if you believe it, you can achieve it. I'm not sure who "they" are, but I'm inclined to agree with them this time. Whatever a mind can conceive can also ultimately be created. With this, we should conceive wisely.

Rest and Recuperation. Step off the scene and take a break for a while, work on yourself, save money, develop your skills, build your business, and brainstorm your brand. Do whatever it takes, but step away for a while. Honestly, when I am done with this publication, I cannot wait to put my devices down and focus on my family, my man, children, elders, and health.

Creating content and building a brand can become a very tedious process, especially when you have been doing it for years. I have been building the same brand since 2012, even though it has evolved significantly over the years. Evolution is necessary for longevity, but I cannot wait to take a break. This book was one of the biggest things on my bucket list. Not too long ago, my family and I took a trip to LA, where I was able to record a song with a Grammy Award-winning artist, producer, and songwriter. That was such a great experience, but it was hard work. That was actually the same week that I found out that I was pregnant, again. Through the share economy, we rented a car and got a cute little hotel family suite in the Disneyland area. Then we hung out in LA for a few days while visiting my dad in Phoenix and just knocked it out. Recording that song was another thing on the bucket list.

With this pending move, creating a new human, master planning, while also living internationally, I feel like the body knows that it is time to take a break. This offering, the artwork, and the website RevolutionaryTravelFamily.com – they are all seeds. I do pray that they grow. I have done everything in my power to promote their growth. The time has come to surrender, on faith.

Recognize when it is time to take a break, reflect on the work you have done, measure your own progress, replenish yourself, and come back rejuvenated. It is time for a personal revival; burnt-out entrepreneurs are not cute. Burnt out moms are not effective. Burnt out life partners are not enjoyable.

We have to allow space and time for regeneration, even if it is a mental rejuvenation. Putting down the phones, pausing the content, halting the consumption, intermittent fasting, and preserving ourselves – we do not need to drain ourselves to the point of exhaustion, working crazy hours, and running around. This has been glamorized for too long; moreover, it has caused far too much disease. If the idea is purpose and impact, how can we do that from a diseased space? Whether mental, physical, or spiritual, how can we fully act out our purpose if our bodies are not functioning correctly? It is important that we take care of ourselves; it is most essential.

Finding our purpose and being able to live it out is the thing that makes life worth living. We did not come to this planet simply to work our youth away until it is time to retire, diseased after we've hoarded all the money, and then die. Life is not about hoarding assets, accumulating, and saving. We have been programmed with that, but that is not the truth. That is not why we came here; that is not why you were born. That is the folder they gave you; that is only the program. However, it is not the purpose; it cannot be.

The purpose is to live life abundantly, be a benefit to those around us, and be a positive influence in the world. We are not to live a wasted life: breathing air, consuming, saving to consume, and living just to pay for a roof over our heads without any purpose in a city that we hate, in a house we've outgrown, with people who do not appreciate us. There was a time when that may have been necessary for survival, and we should show respect and honor for our elders who have paid debts for us; as their elders also made tremendous sacrifices for them.

However, the purpose of evolution is to achieve a higher level of existence for each generation, a higher level of development, and a higher standard of living. We should not pass on the same dysfunctions and debts that we had during our time. That is not evolution, that is not progress, and that is not liberation. That is how crabs remain in a barrel. It should be our duty to **break the barrel**. We should constantly be working to make life better for our downlines. We do not necessarily want life to be easy for our children. We do not want them coddled and unable to handle their responsibilities in adulthood, but they should have access to all available options to be who they want to be. They should not share our same struggles.

Imagine if our grandparents had to share their parents' struggles, some of us may still be on plantations. The world would be a much more primitive place. We should not leave our descendants poisoned environments, destroyed economies, dilapidated infrastructure, all for greed, savings, and instant gratification. That is deferred taxation, it is selfish, and it is evil. We should be leaving a better world for our children to inherit. We should not be making their lives harder before they even had a chance to start. This is why integrity in business and environmental sustainability matters. We should be proactive about every opportunity to "go green."

You do not have to be a tree hugger to figure out that our children will not be able to live on this planet if we continue to sabotage it. Many of the behaviors that we commit in the pursuit of money are not only killing ourselves, but it is directly destroying our future. It is not even giving them a chance. All for what? Money that we cannot take with us and houses and cars that fall apart? Can any of that possibly be more important than our grandchildren's lives?

"Sustainability focuses on meeting the needs of the present without compromising the ability of future generations to meet their needs. The concept of sustainability is composed of three pillars: economic, environmental, and social—also known informally as profits, planet, and people. Increasingly, companies are making public commitments to sustainability through actions like reducing waste, investing in renewable energy, and supporting organizations that work toward a more sustainable future."[87]

Growing Good Fruit. Show honor and respect to our children, as the divine beings they are, raise and guide them, but do not handicap and or misuse them. Mentoring is important. As I wrote before, I don't express this to pretend to be fully healed. Healing is a lifelong journey. Some souls' healing, I believe, spans multiple cycles. If the time has come that we've determined to become our best selves, then healing is definitely taking place.

Harmony and Peace of Mind. To me, at this point, peace of mind has become the highest level of success. I've researched multiple centenarian communities, called Blue Zones, that suggest their long lifespans can be attributed to their lower stress levels, healthier food choices, and a strong sense of community belonging. A centenarian is someone who has lived for at least one hundred years. "Blue Zones are regions of the world where a higher than usual number of people live much longer than average... There are four main things that people in those zones do in order to live healthier and longer lives, and they consist of moving regularly, which does not consist of exercise alone, but doing daily energy burst habits throughout the day. The second aspect is living with purpose, having a reason to get up every day, and living with perspective. The third aspect of blue zone populations is the social support they receive from friends and family allowing them to move through life outcomes more smoothly. Fourth but not least is the concept that most still do not understand, which is making the 'healthy choice the easy choice', and not just an option. Living by these four concepts brings longevity and mental and physical benefits to one's life and society."[88]

Being fully confident that your basic needs are met (like food and shelter), that your loved ones are well cared for, that you are safe and secure, that you have a way to contribute to the whole meaningfully, and your life is being lived with purpose brings one a life-altering sense of peace. For too long, this way of living has been an impossibility for too many. Sometimes the mere idea seems like a crazy daydream. However, if we can shape our reality, we can co-create a world where everyone can live peacefully.

"Creator, help us to walk together in beauty & harmony as one."

Annex: IDEAS

Digitalization, Innovation, & Automation. Large-scale businesses that survive this transition would have to heavily innovate and automate. Small scale businesses will have to focus more on specializing, authenticating, and brand building through the share economy. The self-employed gig worker should continue to build skills and offer services as a specialist, an authority in their field. This would work to their advantage as a starting point, as they would be location-independent and compensated for their time and knowledge, without unnecessary overhead costs of space rentals and products.

Much like the Industrial Revolution of the 1700-1800s, we are currently in the thick of a Technical and Digital Financial Revolution. There are widespread, yet toned-down, discussions of Central Bank Digital Currency (CBDCs) on virtually every continent. Even before the global pandemic, cash was slowly discouraged as a payment method due to contamination issues and limited traceability. International trade, supply chain constraints, and property ownership disputes have made innovation more valued than ever in our lifetime. Meanwhile, thousands of human jobs are being easily replaced with machines requiring zero salary or benefits. A tangible example of this impact can be compared to the decreased need for scribes after the introduction of the printing press.

"Manufacturing is underrated. Design is overrated." (Elon Musk)[89]

Innovate. Manufacturing may be the most complex and time-consuming component of the entire economic process by creating jobs that build skills and provide income, and making actual products that shape social interests and drive demand for currency circulation. Beyond conception and design, we must develop sustainable solutions through which production becomes possible.

It's time for us to do things like they've never been done before (to our knowledge). Even restore older beneficial systems that have been neglected. Creation and sustainability should be a means of ending deferred taxation. What we do right now should only begin to heal the future and not destroy it. We need a totally new shift in mindset regarding the planetary sufferings we're collectively imposing.

With the recognition of these changes, we become aware of a rapidly changing global economy. We could ignore this, continue to consume, and pray for a resumption of business as usual. Or we can prepare to win by planning, building relevant skills, and transforming our lives to benefit from this new future.

There is a **massive** wealth transfer taking place right now, and it is **only our decisions** that determine to which end of the transfer we belong. Literally, it is out with the old, like disintegrating national infrastructures, collapsing financial sectors, decreasing skills for an older labor market, and outdated economic trends. With the new; **anyone** can become a successful investor, university-level courses can be freely found online, high-technology careers now require totally updated skill sets, along with a global shift toward sustainability (instead of only efficiency and capitalism.)

Cryptocurrency. I am eternally thankful for the advent of cryptocurrency. It is literally leveling the playing field for all who choose to participate in the blossoming disruptive financial tool. It is not quick and easy to learn, but it is available to every person on this planet with access to a device with internet capabilities and a desire to learn and benefit from something entirely new. As the previous fiat financial system closes out its cycle, cryptocurrency is already birthing new millionaires and billionaires daily.

These are people with the foresight to notice that this digital financial system is likely here to stay and possess the faith (or riskiness) to put some of their current assets on the line to reap greater gains in the future. Everyone involved today, and still getting involved, is an early adopter. Eventually, it may be mainstream; however, I'm grateful already as it is granting me the ability to live this life with my family. Pre-moonshot!

- Between 2012 and 2020, Bitcoin has gained 193,639.36%
- The first Bitcoin real-life purchase was for two pizzas, and it cost 10,000 BTC.
- The global blockchain market will go up to $23.3 billion by 2023.
- The user index for 2021 shows a 97% confidence in cryptocurrencies.
- The market size for cryptocurrency will reach $1087.7 million by 2026.
- By the end of 2030, banks will save $27 billion through blockchain adoption.
- There were 1000+ US corporate blockchain projects in the pipelines as of late 2020.
- Nigeria was the leading country for cryptocurrency ownership/usage, with 32% in 2020.
- China controls 60% of the world's hash rate[90].[4]
- El Salvador Makes History as the First Country to Accept Bitcoin as Currency

Silver and Gold. Since the beginning of currency, these tangible assets have been a solid investment, no pun intended. They can also serve as a hedge against inflation, especially in this uncertain time. "Human beings have coveted <u>silver</u> and <u>gold</u> consistently for more than 6000 years. Our ancestors used tonnes of silver fashioning valuable ornaments, jewelry, and eating utensils (this in part due to silver's duct ability and natural antibacterial properties). Silver & Gold indeed have the best historic track records as money. These two precious monetary metals, by their inherent natures, are human beings' most excellent monies. Today all physical and digital government issued currencies are fiat, their creation conjured by a computer and printing presses. Their values are based on people's faith and confidence."[91]

Share Economy. I often say that the share economy is one of the best things that ever happened to me. You can find a place to live, rent out a space for someone else to live in, rent a car, and even operate your own car rental service, to name a few. It is really leveling the playing field for everyone who wants to participate in business globally.

- Space rentals (VRBO)
- Vehicle rentals (Turo)
- Pet Sitting (Rover & DogVacay)
- Online shopping communities (Etsy, eBay, Mercari, Poshmark, Shopify)

There are so many ways to make money online these days using platforms such as eBay, Mercari, or Poshmark. They allow you to make a significant profit by selling things you already own but aren't currently using. Shopify also allows you to make stories of your own. While there is a monthly fee, you can easily dropship items depending on the type of store you're running. "Drop shipping is **a fulfillment method where a store doesn't keep the products it sells in stock**. Instead, the store purchases the item from a third-party supplier and has it shipped directly to the customer. As a result, the seller doesn't have to handle the product directly."[92] Drop shipping has made oodles of new school entrepreneurs massively successful without ever touching the items sold.

Crowdfunding. You can raise money for any project you can think of from any person who can contribute through crowdfunding – services like Patreon, Indiegogo, Kickstarter, and GoFundMe. "Crowdfunding is the practice of funding a project or venture by raising small amounts of money from a large number of people, typically via the Internet. Crowdfunding is a form of crowdsourcing and alternative finance." [93]

Build Community. Intentionally cultivating your own circle of influence could be a valuable step. Iron sharpens iron, so you want these people to be sharp. Our family has started The MasterMind Cooperative International Wellness Program for Creatives & Innovators. There will be a strong focus on individuals who have been directly impacted by incarceration. This is just one example of how someone could leverage their passion and build community.

Content Creation. Share your story and use your authentic voice. Content creation is a growing niche for creatives all around the world. This is not a new field as there have been authors, multimedia artists, and all types of creators throughout human history. However, the way things are developing in this new world makes it much easier to monetize your talents no matter how simple they may seem to you now.
- Online Courses
- Skill Sharing (Fiverr)
- Artwork
- YouTube, and such
- Social Media (sponsorships & monetization)

Intellectual Property. "Intellectual property (IP) refers to **creations of the mind**, such as inventions; literary and artistic works; designs; and symbols, names and images used in commerce." [94] I believe that intellectual property is one of the most valuable things that a person can hold. We often discuss generational wealth and value preservation, yet the things you create that can pay you in your lifetime may often benefit more than silver, gold, or even real estate. If you have the time, I seriously suggest looking into developing your own intellectual property. These could include books, music, computer programs, artwork, NFTs, maps, advertisements, films, and more that can draw in recurring income such as royalties. Royalties are **payments to owners of property for use of that property.**[95]

- Trademarks
- Copyrights
- Patents
- Trade Secrets

Keep Reading! Maintain your commitment to reading as if you never got out. Self-education is essential to self-mastery. A person reflects the content of the books they read and the people they're with.

"YOU CAN NEVER FIND FREEDOM OUTSIDE OF YOURSELF." (DEZI)

Below is the **reflection** on the life of a man who has always been there for me. From the time I was born until he died, Uncle Bill was a present contributor. He led a simple life and was unconditionally loyal to those he cared about. I pray that he will never be forgotten.

June 24. 2021

Uncle Bill died yesterday. While the circumstances surrounding his death are still sensitive and uncomfortable, he was tired and did not want to live attached to machines. I have to assess his lifestyle for the many lessons I've garnered. He was a kind man who had been active in my life from the moment I was born; I've never seen him be cruel to a soul. We lived together so often that many people believed he was my father. I was actually beginning to think he may never die because he was just too good of a person and very strong. Someone said, "He never met a stranger," and I wholeheartedly agree. He was not an old man, but a life of poverty and miseducation had left him in poor health. He was also a United States Marine Corps Veteran, a man who kept the family history alive and held what was left of us together. We need good people on this earth. Too many times, we prioritize power, riches, formal education, and such over simple basic goodness. While he was never a religious man, I have no doubt that he is "saved." If sin entails committing harm, he has only harmed himself. He was actively pulling his life together. He enjoyed spending as much time with my children and his grandchildren as he possibly could. He loved HARD and was loyal to no end. Recently, he began to create plans for his future and was collecting his few assets. I'm so upset that he will never be around to repeat his stories or laugh with us again, but I know he has now found absolute peace. I'm learning to value the real things, make more time for those I love, and realize that I don't have to be a superstar to impact and change lives.

No matter how far we make it in life, adulthood becomes a learning process to grieve gracefully. Uncle Bill, Robert Hill, you are Loved Forever. May everyone be blessed with someone like you in their lives.

ABOUT THE AUTHOR

*D*esiree "Dezi Speaks" Riley is a native of Philadelphia, Pennsylvania, with significant ties to Columbus, Ohio. She is a mother, visionary, and creator with a focus on helping to shape this world into a better place for everyone. Dezi graduated from The Ohio State University in 2009, where she worked at the Frank W. Hale Black Cultural Center as a student leader. She also attended Grambling State University and was a member of the University Choir and the Eta Zeta Chapter of Sigma Alpha Iota, International Music Fraternity for Women.

Dezi spends most of her time traveling the globe with her growing family and tending to her work as The Well-Being Specialist. She is also the owner and operator of multiple community-oriented businesses and an entrepreneurship-centered non-profit.

ENDNOTES

1   Mourning Public Enemy #1 Woodland Meadows: https://www.huffpost.com/entry/mourning (accessed November 2, 2021)

2   Choice Definition & Meaning https://www.dictionary.com/browse/choice (accessed August 3, 2021)

3   Thoughts on The Business of Life: https://www.forbes.com/quotes/9383/ (accessed August 3, 2021)

4   Lauren Myrade: Ideas Matter. The World Matters https://www.brainyquote.com/quotes/lauren_myracle_495573 (accessed August 3, 2021)

5   Whatever You Consistently Focus Your Attention On: It Grows http://hypnosis4success.com/whatever-you-consistently-focus-your-attention-on-it-grows/ (accessed August 3, 2021)

6   What You Feed Your Mind: https://www.wow4u.com/mindfeed/ (accessed August 3, 2021)

7   Monika Jensen, Noomii, https://www.noomii.com/articles/6702-whatever-you-consistently-focus-your-attention-on-it-grows (accessed August 3, 2021)

8   "Matthew 18:20," Bible Hub, https://biblehub.com/matthew/18-20.htm (accessed August 10, 2021)

9   Lawrence Krader; Cyril Levitt, Wikipedia, https://en.m.wikipedia.org/wiki/Noetics (accessed August 10, 2021)

10 Institute of Noetic Science, "Defining Noetic Sciences," Noetic https://noetic.org/about/noetic-sciences/ (accessed August 10, 2021)

11 Delorme et al, Noetic, "Collective Consciousness," https://www.google.com/url?q=https://noetic.org (accessed August 10,2021)

12 WebMD, "What is Scarcity Mentality?" WebMD https://www.webmd.com/
mental-health/what-is-scarcity-mentality#:~:text=A%20scarcity%20
mindset%20is%20when,matter%20how%20hard%20you%20try. (accessed
August 12, 2021)

13 Moneyfit MD, "Scarcity Mindset," Moneyfit MD https://www.moneyfitmd.com/
blog/scarcity-mindset (accessed November 2, 2021)

14 Risley Sams, RHS Financial, Money Mindset: From Scarcity
to Abundance: https://rhsfinancial.com/2020/10/15/
money-mindset-from-scarcity-to-abundance/
(accessed August 3, 2021)

15 Matthew B. Gilbert et al, "Breaking Down the Scarcity Mindset," The Harvard
Crimson, May 1, 2020 https://www.thecrimson.com/column/a-time-for-new-
ideas/article/2020 (accessed August 12, 2021)

16 Carolyn C. Milton, "What is Abundant Thinking?" Forbes, April 4, 2018, https://
www.forbes.com/sites/carolyncenteno/2018/04/04/what-is-abundant-
thinking/?sh=23e39bc63a0c (accessed August 12, 2021)

17 Wikipedia, https://en.wikipedia.org/wiki/Abundant_life (accessed August 12,
2021)

18 Jennifer O'Brien Ph. D, "Why Visibility Matters," Psychology Today, November
14, 2017,
https://www.psychologytoday.com/us/blog/all-things-lgbtq/201711/
why-visibility-matters (accessed August 12, 2021)

19 DBpedia, "Self- Esteem," https://dbpedia.org/page/Self-esteem (accessed
August 12, 2021)

20 Michael Blosser, "Practicing Applying Newton's Third Law," Study.com, https://
study.com/academy/lesson/practice-applying-newton-s-third-law.html
(accessed August 12, 2021)

21 Wikipedia, "Newton's Laws of Motion," https://en.wikipedia.org/wiki/
Newton%27s_laws_of_motion (accessed August 3, 2021)

22 J.E.B. Spredemann, "An Unforgivable Secret," Goodreads
https://www.goodreads.com/quotes/839174-choices-made-whether-bad-or-
good-follow-you-forever-and (accessed August 3, 2021)

23 Wikipedia, "Karma," https://en.wikipedia.org/wiki/Karma (accessed August 3, 2021)

24 "How people treat you is their karma. How you react is yours." PassItOn, https://www.passiton.com/inspirational-quotes/6455-how-people-treat-you-is-their-karma-how-you#:~:text=%E2%80%9CHow%20people%20treat%20you%20is,Wayne%20Dyer%20%7C%20PassItOn.com (accessed August 3, 2021)

25 "Maharishi Mahesh Yogi Quotes," BrainyQuote https://www.brainyquote.com/quotes/maharishi_mahesh_yogi_556190#:~:text=Maharishi%20Mahesh%20Yogi%20Quotes&text=Problems%20or%20successes%2C%20they%20all%20are%20the%20results%20of%20our,happiness%20or%20success%20or%20whatever (accessed August 3, 2021)

26 "Angie Stone Quotes," BrainyQuote https://www.google.com/url?q=https://www.brainyquote.com/quotes/angie_stone_234926 (accessed August 3, 2021)

27 "Proverbs 1:31," BibleHub, Biblica Inc, https://biblehub.com/proverbs/1-31.htm (accessed August 3, 2021)

28 "Quote by Robert G. Ingersoll," Good Reads, https://www.goodreads.com/quotes/50079-there-are-in-nature-neither-rewards-nor-punishments-there (accessed August 3, 2021)

29 "Galatians 6:7 - 8," Biblia, https://biblia.com/bible/nkjv/galatians/6/7-8 (accessed August 3, 2021)

30 "The Golden Rule is Universal," Golden Rule Project, https://www.goldenruleproject.org/formulations#:~:text=%E2%80%9COne%20should%2 (accessed August 3, 2021)

31 Ahadi, "Quran surah Ash shura 30 (QS 42: 30) in arabic and english translation," AlquranEnglish, July 1, 2009 https://www.alquranenglish.com/quran-surah-ash-shura-30-qs-42-30-in-arabic-and-english-translation (accessed August 3, 2021)

32 Jan Thomas, "Vedanta: The Oneness of All," Jan Thomas - Soul and Meaning, Soul and Meaning, February 27,2018 https://www.google.com/url?q=https://soulandmeaning.com/vedanta-the-oneness-of-all

(accessed August 3, 2021)

33   "For Peace against the fog and blood of war," Google Books, https://books. google.com/books?id=hJK8DwAAQBAJ&lpg=PA3&ots=JtJc66Hnfi&dq =O%20seeker%2C%20know%20the%20true%20nature%20of%20your%20 soul%2C%20and%20identify%20yourself%20with%20it%20completely.%20 O%20Lord%2C%20(may%20we%20attain)%20the%20everlasting%20 consciousness%20of%20Supreme%20Light%20and%20Joy.%20May%20 we%20resolve%20to%20dedicate%20our%20life%20to%20the%20 service%20of%20humankind%2C%20and%20uplift%20them%20to%20 Divinity.%20(Yajur%20Veda)&pg=PA3#v=onepage&q=O%20seeker,%20 know%20the%20true%20nature%20of%20your%20soul,%20and%20 identify%20yourself%20with%20it%20completely.%20O%20Lord,%20 (may%20we%20attain)%20the%20everlasting%20consciousness%20of%20 Supreme%20Light%20and%20Joy.%20May%20we%20resolve%20to%20 dedicate%20our%20life%20to%20the%20service%20of%20humankind,%20 and%20uplift%20them%20to%20Divinity.%20(Yajur%20Veda)&f=false (accessed August 3, 2021)

34   "Gustave Flaubert", AZ Quotes, Wind and Fly Ltd, https://www.azquotes.com/ quote/97444?ref=consequ (accessed August 9, 2021)

35   "#7 Emotional Content" Bruce Lee's Wisdom for a Harmonious Life, https:// brucelee.com/podcast-blog/2016/8/24/7-emotional-content (accessed August 9, 2021)

36   Dave Kerpen, "15 Inspiring Quotes on Passion (Get Back to What You Love)," INC, March 27, 2014, https://www.inc.com/dave-kerpen/15-quotes-on-passion-to-inspire-a-better-life.html (accessed August 9, 2021).

37   Sam McNerney, "Where Does Passion Come From?" The Creativity Post, June 2, 2012, https://www.google.com/url?q=https://www.creativitypost.com/article/ where_does_passi (accessed August 10, 2021)

38   Plummer, Bryan. "The future belongs to those who prepare for it today," Amandala Newspaper, July 22, 2020 https://www.google.com/ url?q=https://amandala.com.bz/news/the-future-belongs-to-thos (accessed November 2, 2021)

39 "Rita Mae Brown" GoodReads, https://www.goodreads.com/quotes/87111-good-judgment-comes-from-experience-and-experience-comes-from-bad (accessed August 3, 2021)

40 Paul Koptak, "What is the Difference Between Wisdom and Knowledge," Got Questions, https://www.gotquestions.org/wisdom-knowledge.html (accessed August 3 2021)

41 "Drew Barrymore Quotes," BrainyQuote, https://www.brainyquote.com/quotes/drew_barrymore_600077 (accessed August 3, 2021)

42 Erykah Badu. "The Healer," Track 2 on New Amerykah, Pt. 1: 4th World War, Motown Records, 2008 https://www.google.com/url?q=https://genius.com/Erykah-badu-the-healer-lyrics&sa=D& (accessed August 3, 2021)

43 The Black History Month Project, "Marcus Garvey: National Hero of Jamaica," The Black History Month Project, WordPress, https://theblackhistorymonthproject.wordpress.com/2012/02/02/marcus-garvey-national-hero-of-jamaica/ (accessed August 3, 2021)

44 Debomitra Das, "How Childhood Trauma Can Affect Your Relationships," Entertainment Times, Times of India, https://www.google.com/url?q=https://timesofindia.indiatimes.com/life-style/relationships(accessed August 10, 2021)

45 International Society for Traumatic Stress Studies, "Trauma and Relationships," ISTSS, https://istss.org/ISTSS_Main/media/Documents/ISTSS_TraumaAndRelationships_FNL.pdf (accessed August 10, 2021)

46 "How Childhood Trauma Affects Us as Adults," Mental Health Center, June 7, 2016 https://www.mentalhealthcenter.org/how-childhood-trauma-affects-adult-relationships/ (accessed August 10, 2021)

47 Dr, Todd Thatcher, "Can Emotional Trauma Cause Brain Damage," Highland Springs Clinic, February 4, 2019, https://www.google.com/url?q=https://highlandspringsclinic.org/blog/can-emotional-trauma-cause-brain-damage/&sa=D&source=docs&ust=1638281998244000&usg=AOvVaw1BJyrN1yBdflsiCi6wUGYL (accessed August 10, 2021)

48 "Charles F. Kettering Quotes," QuoteFancy, https://quotefancy.com/quote/785225/Charles-F-Kettering-One-fails-forward-toward-success (accessed August 3, 2021)

49 "Romans 8 NIV," Bible Hub, Biblica Inc, https://biblehub.com/niv/romans/8. htm (accessed August 3, 2021)

50 "Napoleon Hill Quotes," BrainyQuotes, https://www.brainyquote.com/quotes/napoleon_hill_258565 (accessed August 3,2021)

51 Selina Eng Rui, "The Tony Robbins CAN! System for Success," Ezine Articles, March 24, 2009, https://ezinearticles.com/?The-Tony-Robbins-CAN!-System-For-Success&id=2136102 (accessed August 10, 2021)

52 Marshall Hargrave, "Kaizen Definition," Investopedia, https://www. investopedia.com/terms/k/kaizen.asp# (accessed August 10, 2021)

53 Xiang Zhou; Samma Faiz Rasool; Jing Yang; Muhammad Zaheer Asghar, "Exploring the Relationship between Despotic Leadership and Job Satisfaction: The Role of Self Efficacy and Leader-Member Exchange," Int J Environ Res Public Health, May 18,2021, https://www.ncbi.nlm.nih.gov/pmc/articles/PMC8155868/#:~:text=2.3.-,Self%2DEfficacy%20(SE),perform%20certain%20tasks%20%5B30%5D (accessed August 10, 2021)

54 "Self-efficacy," Psynso, https://psynso.com/self-efficacy/ (accessed August 12, 2021)

55   Michael Carey; Andrew Forsyth, "Teaching Tip Sheet: Self Efficacy," American Psychological Association, https://www.apa.org/pi/aids/resources/education/self-efficacy#:~:text=Self%2Defficacy%20refers%20to%20an,%2C%20behavior%2C%20and%20social%20environment (accessed August 10, 2021)

56 Abigail Rolston; Elizabeth Lloyd Richardson, "What is emotion regulation and how do we do it?" Cornell Research Program on Self-Injury and Recovery, http://www.selfinjury.bctr.cornell.edu/perch/resources/what-is-emotion-regulationsinfo-brief.pdf (accessed August 12, 2021)

57 Mark Follows, "Want Accountability In the Workplace? Do this, or else," Carpedia, May 11, 2021, https://carpedia.com/blog/want-accountability-in-the-workplace-do-this-or-else/ (accessed August 12, 2021)

58 "Accountability breeds response-ability," Rock Solid Business Development, https://rocksolidbizdevelopment.com/ourblog/accountability-breeds-response-ability/ (accessed August 3, 2021)

59   Sandy Gallagher, "Accountability," Proctor Gallagher Institute, https://www. proctorgallagherinstitute.com/17557/accountability (accessed August 3, 2021)

60   "Luke 6:42," Bible Hub, Biblica Inc, https://biblehub.com/luke/6-42.htm (accessed August 3, 2021)

61   John Drury, "Why it's important to have self-respect in life and at work," HRM: The news site of the Australian HR Institute, October 6,2017, https:// www.hrmonline.com.au/section/strategic-hr/important-self-respect-life-work/#:~:text=It%20means%20knowing%20what%20you,and%20 knowing%20how%20to%20rebuild (accessed August 12, 2021)

62   Carol Dweck, Mindset - Updated Edition: Changing The Way You think To Fulfill Your Potential, (Little, Brown Book Group, 2017) (accessed August 12, 2021)

63   Carol Dweck, "What Having a "Growth Mindset" Actually Means," Harvard Business Reviews, January 13, 2016, https://hbr.org/2016/01/what-having-a-growth-mindset-actually-means (accessed August 10, 2021)

64   "Fears and Phobias (for teens)," Nemours Teens Health, https://kidshealth.org/en/teens/phobias.html (accessed August 12, 2021)

65   Jeremy Sherman, "Fear of Inadequacy and What to Do About It," Psychology Today, July 25, 2016, https://www.psychologytoday.com/us/blog/ambigamy/201607/fear-inadequacy-and-what-do-about-it (accessed August 12, 2021)

66   "Fear Proverbs," Proverbicals, https://proverbicals.com/fear (accessed August 3, 2021)

67   "The Art of Mastery," Blatchford Solutions Business Consulting for Dentists, https://blatchford.com/resources/dental-practice-management-articles/the-art-of-mastery/ (accessed August 12, 2021)

68   Kendra Cherry, "Self-Determination Theory and Motivation," March 15, 2021, https://www.verywellmind.com/what-is-self-determination-theory-2795387#:~:text=In%20psychology%2C%20self%2Ddetermination%20 is,over%20their%20choices%20and%20lives (accessed August 12, 2021)

69   "Ashish Patel Quotes," Good Reads, https://www.goodreads.com/author/quotes/10211736.Ashish_Patel#:~:text=%E2%80%9CThe%20elegance%20 under%20pressure%20is%20the%20result%20of%20fearlessness.%E2%

80%9D&text=%E2%80%9CFormal%20education%20and%20current%20 position,by%20your%20attitude%20towards%20others.%E2%80%9D (accessed August 3, 2021)

70 "Confidence," Psychology Today, https://www.psychologytoday.com/us/ basics/confidence (accessed August 12, 2021)

71 "Hustle," The Free Dictionary by Farlex, https://www.thefreedictionary.com/ hustles (accessed August 12, 2021)

72 "James Clear on Twitter," Twitter, https://twitter.com/jamesclear/status/122742 0216398925824?lang=en (accessed September 9, 2021)

73 "Ten Rules for Profitable Self Discipline," Wealth Forum Online, June 11, 2015, http://wealthforumonline.com/bible-and-wealth/ten-rules-for-profitable-self-discipline/ (accessed August 9, 2021)

74 "Don't spend your major time on minor things," ReadBeach, https://readbeach. com/quote/don-t-spend-your-major-time-on-minor-things (accessed August 24, 2021)

75 "Thoughts on the Business of Life," Forbes Quotes, Forbes, https://www.forbes. com/quotes/6764/ (accessed August 3, 2021)

76 Michael Holshouser, "Definition: An Incomplete Selection of Contemplative Definitions," https://www.google.com/url?q=http://www. thestillnessbeforetime.com/definitions.pdf&sa=D&source=docs&ust=16383 93781575000&usg=AOvVaw2w2RMZXslAMFb1mupHbhEr (accessed August 10, 2021)

77 R. Prasad, "Explained: How do oxygen levels affect cell metabolism?" The Hindu, October 13, 2019, https://www.thehindu.com/sci-tech/science/how-oxygen-levels-affect-cell-metabolism/article29668134.ece/amp/ (accessed August 10, 2021)

78 Danny Penman, "Can You Reduce Anxiety and Stress by the Way You Breathe?" Psychology Today, June 27 2018, https://www.psychologytoday.com/us/blog/ mindfulness-in-frantic-world/201806/can-you-reduce-anxiety-and-stress-the-way-you-breathe (accessed August 10, 2021)

79 Mark Michaud-Rochester, "Capillaries Scramble to Feed Oxygen to Brain," Futurity, August 10, 2016, https://www.futurity.org/brain-oxygen-energy-1221902-2/ (accessed August 10, 2021)

80   Healthwise Staff, "How the Heart Works," Alberta, August 31, 2020 https://myhealth.alberta.ca/Health/Pages/conditions.aspx?hwid=tx4097abc (accessed August 10, 2021)

80   Susan Sun Nunamaker, "Lessons for Longevity From Centenarians," Windermere Sun, June 8, 2021, https://www.windermeresun.com/2021/06/08/lessons-for-lonevity-from-centenarians/ (accessed August 10, 2021)

81   "Eric Hoffer:Quotes," Brittanica, https://www.britannica.com/quotes/biography/Eric-Hoffer (accessed August 3, 2021)

82   Olivier Poirier-Leroy, "3 Unappreciated Benefits of the Struggle," Swim Swam, September 30, 2015, https://swimswam.com/3-underappreciated-benefits-of-the-struggle/ (accessed August 10, 2021)

83   "Proverbs 29:18," Bible Gateway, https://www.biblegateway.com/passage/?search=Proverbs%2029%3A18&version=KJV (accessed August 3, 2021)

84   Peter Medawar Quote," AZ Quotes, https://www.azquotes.com/quote/531790 (accessed August 3, 2021)

85   "Where there is no vision, the people perish," The Thursday Thought, Medium, https://medium.com/thethursdaythought/where-there-is-no-vision-the-people-perish-3c22c5f730cd (accessed August 3, 2021)

86   Bob Proctor, "If You Can Hold It In Your Head, You Can Hold It In Your Hand," with Sean Croxton, The Quote of the Day| Daily Motivational Talks

87   Daniel Thomas Mollenkamp, "Sustainability Definition," Investopedia, https://www.investopedia.com/terms/s/sustainability.asp (accessed August 12, 2021)

88   Dan Buettner, "Longevity: Secrets of Long Life," National Geographic, https://web.archive.org/web/20170530005432/http://ngm.nationalgeographic.com/ngm/0511/feature1/ (accessed August 10, 2021)

89   Elon Musk, "Starbase Tour with Elon Musk [PART 1]," interview by Tim Dodd. YouTube, August 3, 2021

90   Jacquelyn Bulao, "44 Amazing Cryptocurrency Statistics You Need to Know," TechJury, https://techjury.net/blog/cryptocurrency-statistics/#gref (accessed August 3, 2021)

91   "The History of Silver & Gold," JM Bullion, https://www.jmbullion.com/investing-guide/james/gold-silver-history/ (accessed August 10, 2021)

92   Corey Ferreira, "What is Dropshipping?" Shopify Blog, June 2, 2021, https://www.shopify.com/blog/what-is-dropshipping#:~:text=Dropshipping%20is%20a%20fulfillment%20method,to%20handle%20the%20product%20directly, (accessed August 10, 2021)

93   Goran Calic, "Crowd Funding," The SAGE Encyclopedia of the Internet, SAGE Pub, https://sk.sagepub.com/reference/the-sage-encyclopedia-of-the-internet-3v/i1840.xml (accessed August 10, 2021)

94   "What Is Intellectual Property?" WIPO, https://www.wipo.int/about-ip/en/ (accessed August 10, 2021)

95   Jean Murray, "Royalties: What Are They?" The Balance Small Business, June 29, 2020, https://www.thebalancesmb.com/what-are-royalties-how-they-work-4142673#:~:text=Royalties%20are%20payments%20to%20owners,copyrights%2C%20patents%2C%20and%20trademarks, (accessed August 10, 2021)

www.ingramcontent.com/pod-product-compliance
Lightning Source LLC
Chambersburg PA
CBHW071354120626
46546CB00002B/683